Praise for *Jesus Revolution*

"For those who were eyewitnesses to the Jesus Movement, this book will be a welcome reminder of what made that time of our lives so special. For those who know nothing about it, this book will be an entertaining crash course on events that defined the Christian church in America for generations. For everyone, it will be a compelling testimony about the power of God to save."

Dr. Jack Graham, pastor, Prestonwood Baptist Church

"*The Jesus Revolution* has tuned my heart to a higher level of praise for a loving God who has the proven power to break through to a lost, godless, self-destructing generation and redeem it, one person at a time. If He could rescue and reset Greg Laurie—and He did—then there is no one and no generation beyond His reach. Reading this book will rekindle your prayer for revival."

Anne Graham Lotz, speaker; author, *The Daniel Prayer*;
www.annegrahamlotz.org

"Back in the '60s, when I first came to Christ, you could sense a stirring out on the West Coast. God was on the move, and I was about to be swept up in the powerful flooding of the Holy Spirit that was spilling and splashing into the hearts of a million young people across America. I heard stories of how God was rescuing wayward wanderers through the Jesus Movement, sparking a revival that rocked our country and beyond. It's why Greg and Ellen's new book, *Jesus Revolution*, is so important, so needed—it documents the testimonies and events that made that period in time so unique. You, too, will be inspired and refreshed as you read the historic account of one of the most remarkable seasons of revival in the history of Christianity!"

Joni Eareckson Tada, Joni and Friends
International Disability Center

"In the 1960s and '70s, God moved in a unique way, sweeping across America and transforming the lives of countless people. In their new book, *Jesus Revolution*, Pastor Greg Laurie and Ellen Vaughn take a closer look at this incredible time of evangelism and revival. This fast-paced, grace-filled, Bible-centered book will show you how God uses ordinary people to do extraordinary things."

Craig Groeschel, pastor, Life.Church;
New York Times bestselling author

"Greg Laurie and Ellen Vaughn have given us a compelling and insightful look into the Jesus Movement of the '60s and '70s. As our society seems to grow more and more dark, this book makes me excited and hopeful that maybe we are not that far from another great move of God."

Chris Tomlin, music artist, songwriter, author

"Revival is a mile marker that is seen throughout the centuries, with the Jesus Movement being no exception. Greg Laurie and Ellen Vaughn have given us a riveting account of a time in our nation's history when God uniquely captivated millions of hearts. This book will stir up a fresh gratitude for what God has done and a renewed hunger to see Him do even more in the years to come!"

Levi Lusko, bestselling author, *Swipe Right: The Life-and-Death Power of Sex and Romance*

"So few even realize today that many of the best things happening in our churches amount only to ripples from the 1970s revival wave called the Jesus Revolution. Greg Laurie was an eyewitness to what most have only heard about. His meaningful firsthand accounts flow through Ellen Vaughn's gripping narrative, prompting every reader to cry out, 'Do it again, Lord.' Read and join those already praying to see God move afresh in such powerful ways."

Dr. James MacDonald, founder, Harvest Bible Chapel; author, *Vertical Church*

"If there was ever a time that a book like this was needed, it is now. The story of the Jesus Revolution is a compelling witness of God's power to redeem and restore human souls in the most surprising of ways, in the most chaotic of times. Brilliant work, Greg and Ellen!"

Dr. Robert Jeffress, senior pastor, First Baptist Church, Dallas, Texas; teacher, Pathway to Victory

"Stories inspire people to believe God. This is why I am so excited about this powerful book about the Jesus Revolution, because I know it will create the spiritual appetite to experience the next great move of God in our generation. There is no greater need today than for the church to be revived spiritually and for the next great spiritual awakening to occur nationally. Now is the time for the next Jesus Revolution in America!"

Dr. Ronnie Floyd, senior pastor, Cross Church; president, National Day of Prayer; past president, Southern Baptist Convention

"Rarely have I read a book so entertaining, informative, and spiritually significant as *Jesus Revolution*. I relived many formative historical events of the '60s and '70s and learned new and fascinating things about the Jesus Movement. I can't think of anyone better than Greg Laurie to be a central character and voice, nor anyone better than Ellen Vaughn to skillfully craft this fascinating story of a powerful movement of the Holy Spirit. I loved it, and I pray God would do such radical works of grace in our midst today!"

Randy Alcorn, author, *Heaven*
and *The Grace & Truth Paradox*

GREG LAURIE

with *LARRY LIBBY*

BakerBooks

a division of Baker Publishing Group
Grand Rapids, Michigan

Published by Baker Books
a division of Baker Publishing Group
PO Box 6287, Grand Rapids, MI 49516-6287
www.bakerbooks.com

Printed in the United States of America

Library of Congress Cataloging-in-Publication Control Number: 2020003663

ISBN 978-0-8010-7595-7

The author is represented by the literary agency of Wolgemuth & Associates, Inc.

20 21 22 23 24 25 26   7 6 5 4 3 2 1

To Charles Spurgeon,
D. L. Moody,
G. Campbell Morgan,
Alan Redpath,
Chuck Smith,
Chuck Swindoll,
and, of course,
Billy Graham.
All world changers
who changed my world.

Contents

Introduction

"Lord, Please Use Me Today"

I wasn't raised in the church or anywhere near it, so I never really understood that there was a God who loved me and had a plan for my life. Then at the age of seventeen—on my high school campus of all places—I heard someone articulate the plan of salvation in a way that suddenly made sense to me, and I put my trust in Jesus Christ.

To this day, I can recall the sense of wonder and amazement I felt as I tried to get my arms around a huge, incredible reality. The great God and Creator of the whole universe actually loved and cared about a fatherless kid named Greg Laurie.

That was mind-blowing enough for me. But as the days went by, I also learned that this same God wanted to use me. *Me!* I was only two weeks old in my commitment to Christ and knew next to nothing about the Bible or the Christian life, but I had heard that I should go out and share the gospel with others. So one day I stuffed some gospel tracts in my pocket and went down to the beach—the same beach where

I used to make a point of avoiding any Bible-toting Christians who might try to convert me.

Now here I was—a bona fide member of the "soul patrol"—out prowling for unbelievers to convert. But I wasn't exactly full of confidence. In fact, my main goal was to find someone who wouldn't argue or get angry at me. I thought if an unbeliever just ignored me or walked away, that would be fine.

Eventually, I spotted a middle-aged lady who looked about the age of my mom. I figured she might be somewhat sympathetic to me. When I walked up to her, my voice trembled with nervousness. "Uh, excuse me," I said, fumbling for the right words. "Can I talk to you about something?"

She said, "Sure. What about?"

"Well, about, like, God—and stuff," I answered. (Remember, I was still a teenager.)

To my amazement, she said, "Go ahead. Sit down. Talk to me."

I pulled out one of the evangelistic tracts I had stuffed in my pocket for a moment like this. I was so new in the faith that I hadn't even memorized the plan of salvation, so I just read through the entire tract verbatim. The whole time I read, I was shaking like a leaf and thinking, *This isn't going to work. Why am I doing this? This is not going to reach her.* But the woman continued to patiently listen to what I was saying—rather, reading.

When I got to a part in the presentation that said, "Is there any good reason why you shouldn't accept Jesus Christ right now?" I realized that I should direct this question to the woman. I hesitated. Feeling awkward, I looked up and asked her, "Uh, is there any good reason why you should not accept Jesus Christ right now?"

"No," she replied.

"Okay," I said, slightly confused. "Then that would mean that you *do* want to accept Jesus Christ right now?"

With a look of quiet resolve, she answered, "Yes, I would."

I was shocked. For a moment I didn't know what to do. I had only planned for failure. Frantically I searched the tract for some kind of prayer in which to lead a person who wanted to invite Christ into his or her life. After what seemed like an eternity, I finally found one. In the most reverent tone I could muster, I said, "Let's bow our heads for a word of prayer."

Even as she prayed after me, I was still thinking, *This isn't going to work*. After we were done, the woman looked up at me and said, "Something just happened to me!"

And at that moment something happened to me too. I got a taste of what it was like to be used by God. I knew—even at that point, at that young age—that no matter what I did in life, I wanted to continue to share the gospel.

Like most people, I had a strong fear of public speaking. You have probably heard that whenever studies are done about fear, people usually put public speaking as number one—sometimes even before death. Even so, I began to get the strong message from the Lord that He wanted me, teenager Greg Laurie, to *preach*.

Before I became a Christian, I remember hanging out at the beach in Corona Del Mar in Newport Beach in Southern California and running into a rather unusual guy who would stand in the blazing sun and tell everyone to repent of their sins and turn to Jesus. He was dressed completely in black—head to toe—and he seemed as strange to me as a space alien. I stood there in my board shorts and T-shirt thinking, *If there's one person in the world I would never want to be, it's* that *guy.*

Years later, as a brand-new Christian, I found myself standing on the same beach in Corona Del Mar, almost in the same spot where the crazy preacher dressed in black had stood. I shared the gospel with a group of girls, they all accepted the Lord, and I baptized them in the ocean. After that, I walked by a group of people who were up on the cliffs at Corona.

The Lord spoke to me and said, "Preach."

Preach? Me? But Lord, I don't know the Bible. What if someone asks me a question? I don't even know how to do this.

I heard His voice again, saying, "Preach."

So I preached. And what could have been the most terrifying moment of my life became the most exciting and exhilarating. God actually picked me up and used me to preach to a group of total strangers that day, and it was a huge turning point in my young life.

It gave me the hope that somehow, some way, in some measure, He would change the world through me.

The truth is, God wants to use every one of us as a world changer. It may not be a matter of standing in front of people and declaring His message—that was His challenge to me. But it may very well mean leaving our comfort zones and stretching our faith to attempt something we have never done before.

A good way to begin stepping into a new place in your life is to pray a simple prayer like this: *God, I will do what You want me to do, go where You want me to go, and say what You want me to say.* And then just stay alert for opportunities to step out in faith as the Lord opens doors for you.

All of us need to be praying about how God can use us to change our world, because every Christian is called to serve

God. This call to be available to the Lord isn't just for preachers, missionaries, evangelists, or people in full-time ministry. Every Christian has a part to play and a role to serve.

I love Paul's words in Romans 12:4–6: "Just as our bodies have many parts and each part has a special function, so it is with Christ's body. We are many parts of one body, and we all belong to each other. In his grace, God has given us different gifts for doing certain things well" (NLT).

We're all parts of this one body and each of us has different work to do. And since we are all one body in Christ, we belong to each other and each of us needs all the others. So what does that look like? Maybe something like this.

When you first open your eyes in the morning, before you put your feet on the floor, offer up a silent prayer: *Lord, use me.*

When you walk through the doors of your church: *Lord, use me.*

When you enter your workplace or classroom or step into a coffee shop to meet a friend: *Lord, use me.*

When you step through your front door into your house with your own family: *Lord, use me.*

I can assure you with all confidence that God is looking for people to use every day, people who want to serve others rather than be served. As the Old Testament prophet told King Asa, "The eyes of the LORD search the whole earth in order to strengthen those whose hearts are fully committed to him" (2 Chron. 16:9 NLT). God will use you if you let Him.

Sometimes people make excuses like, "Well, Greg, you have an opportunity to write books, speak in stadiums full of people, and stand behind that supercool lighted pulpit at your church. I don't have a pulpit like that." Actually, you do have a pulpit. It doesn't have to be like mine. A pulpit is simply a platform, an opportunity, a sphere of influence no matter who you are or where you are. If you flip burgers in a fast-food place, you have a pulpit. If you wash dishes in a restaurant, you have a pulpit. If you drive a taxi or Uber, you have a pulpit. If you're a business executive, you have a pulpit. If you are a prisoner on work release, you have a pulpit.

A world changer is simply an individual—man, woman, or even a child—who makes the daily choice to allow God to use him or her in whatever way He sees fit. And believe me on this, that sort of determination can lead you into places and situations and conversations you never would have dreamed possible! I can attest to that truth, and so could the biblical heroes named in Hebrews 11—the chapter Bible students through the years have called "the Hall of Faith." In the pages to follow, we will explore their stories. These are men and women who, through tenacious faith in God, made difficult choices and took unpopular stands that went directly against the culture of the day. In so doing, they marked their world for God, and their stories have been told for thousands of years.

But before we talk about them let's dive into a much more contemporary example. Not long ago I received this letter from a public schoolteacher in our area.

Dear Pastor Greg,

I'm a high school teacher in a pretty tough area. As a public schoolteacher, I have to find creative ways of witnessing to the students and sharing the love of Jesus with them—because Jesus is a very foreign concept to many of the students here. So I decided to give the students an extra credit assignment over the weekend. They had to watch the Anaheim Harvest Crusade on TV or go to the Crusade in person and then do a one-page write-up on what they saw or experienced. I am happy to report that a few of the students gave their lives to Jesus. Several more were asking me questions, which is an awesome opportunity to plant more seeds.

The Crusade got many of the students thinking about things they had never heard about in their homes. My prayer is that those who saw the Crusade and haven't made a decision for Christ will make the final decision. No matter what, I'll keep in contact with those kids and continue to be a witness to them.

Now that's a man who knows what his pulpit is. Yes, I suppose in today's culture he was taking a career risk. But he saw an opportunity, stepped forward in faith, and let God use him. In doing so, he is changing his world.

If we learn anything from these reflections on the Hebrews 11 Hall of Faith, it's that these people were far from perfect. They didn't end up in this New Testament honor roll because they were such holy, wise, or super talented men and women. No, they have become examples to us for one reason. At some point in their lives, in some situation or crisis in which they found themselves, they chose to step out of their comfort zones, exercise their faith, and make themselves available to the almighty God.

We can all think of plenty of reasons why God could never use us. And if we can't dredge up reasons on our own, Satan will be glad to assist us. Just think about some of the Bible heroes and their stumbles.

The great patriarch Abraham, stumbled in his faith—twice—telling lies in the bargain. Sarah, his wife, laughed at God's promise and then denied it. Jacob lied, cheated, and connived. Noah got drunk and put himself in a compromising position. Samson was a woman chaser and a very immoral man. Gideon struggled with fear and self-doubt. Rahab was a prostitute. Elijah struggled with depression and even wanted to die. David had an affair and committed murder. Jonah ran from God. The Samaritan woman had multiple divorces. The disciples fell asleep praying. Peter denied even knowing Jesus. And Lazarus was dead. *So what's your excuse?*

Think about it. These people either had an excuse or messed up in major ways. But God gave them second chances to serve Him. Maybe you need a second chance as you are reading this book. Maybe you have had a lapse of faith along your journey. You're like that lady in the Life Alert commercial: "Help! I've fallen and I can't get up!"

But that's not true, is it? You can get up, you can have a second chance, and God can still use you right where you are in life. *Get up and run again.* If you are still breathing as you read these words, your story isn't over. That's what Hebrews 11 is all about. And what is the one key that enabled these failing men and women to change the world?

One word: faith.

The key is faith.

Are You a World Changer?

> Faith is the confidence that what we hope for will actually happen; it gives us assurance about things we cannot see.
>
> ~Hebrews 11:1 NLT

I don't know how it is in your house, but under the Laurie roof my wife and I tend toward minor disagreements—I won't say arguments—about room temperature.

Let me cut to the chase here. Cathe likes it warm—*really* warm—and I like it cool. Sometimes in the winter months I may find myself breaking out in a sweat as we're hanging out in the living room, reading or watching TV. After walking over to check out the thermostat, I will invariably find it set at 78.

78!

"Cathe," I will protest, "why did you set the temperature so high?"

"I was cold."

"I'm actually sweating! I think I've dropped four pounds in this heat."

"But wouldn't that be a good thing?"

While I'm up, I will take the opportunity to reset the temperature at a comfortable and more logical 70. I like 70—70 is good for me. I'm pretty sure the temperature in the garden of Eden was 70, and no one was wearing sweaters either.

Really our disagreements are just a little fruitless. Cathe likes it warmer, and Greg likes it cooler. So we go back to the thermostat again and again, adjusting each other's adjustments. Why do we find ourselves so often at the thermostat? Because that's the device that controls the temperature of the room.

With this in mind, I have a question for you. Are you a thermostat or are you a thermometer? You might be thinking, *What are you talking about, Greg? I'm a person, not a device on the wall.* True. But it all comes down to this. You and I can be like thermometers or we can be like thermostats. A thermometer is affected by its surroundings; it follows changes in the temperature, as the marker rises or falls. *A thermometer simply reflects what is already there.* By contrast, a thermostat influences or controls its surroundings. It can take a hot room and make it cool, or it can start with a cold room and warm it up. *A thermostat adjusts the conditions of its environment.*

So which are you, a thermometer or a thermostat?

Let me put it another way. Are you changing the culture around you, or is culture changing you? Is the world adjusting you, or are you adjusting the world?

A Tall Order

In the pages of this book we will look together at stories of great men and women who served the Lord in their own generations and, in real ways—great and small—actually changed their world.

They could have been thermometers, rising or falling with the culture and the times, dutifully reflecting the customs and circumstances around them. If so, we would have never read about them. History is full of thermometers. The people we will read about in this book, however, were thermostats—thousands of years before Albert Butz of the Honeywell Corporation invented the first one in 1885.

They were world changers. And as we learn from their examples and follow in their footsteps, by God's grace and in His strength, we can be world changers too.

Change the world? You might be thinking that's a pretty tall order. Yes, but what about *your* world? What about *your* sphere of influence? *Your* friends, family, and neighborhood? *Your* workplace, school, or dorm? What about under your very own roof? You can have an effect there. You can be the change agent. The thermostat. The world changer.

How do you do it? How do you change your immediate environment for the better?

You do it through faith. And that's the theme of this book.

Rock Stars of the Faith

A number of years ago I was in New York City, and I visited a rock and roll hall of fame exhibit. They had some interesting items, including John Lennon's all-white piano on which he composed his song "Imagine." They also had Jimi Hendrix's couch (though I think I would have been more interested in his guitar). On multiple screens you could watch videos of various rock stars performing their music or just clowning around.

As we open the eleventh and twelfth chapters of Hebrews, you might want to think of those listed in terms of "rock stars of the faith." These are people who changed their world—and in doing so, changed our world too. I'm talking about people like Abraham, Enoch, Noah, Sarah, Joseph, Moses . . . and the list goes on.

The author of Hebrews begins chapter 12 with the words: "Therefore we also, since we are surrounded by so great a cloud of witnesses . . . let us run with endurance the race that is set before us, looking unto Jesus, the author and finisher of our faith" (vv. 1, 2).

That cloud of witnesses he refers to is the men and women who inhabit the Hall of Faith in chapter 11. These were ordinary people like you and me who somehow changed their world. Think of it! Thousands of years later—after scores of world empires have risen and crumbled into the dust—we're still thinking about them, talking about them, and telling their stories.

How did they find the secret of making such a stunning difference—a difference that would have lasting impact centuries later? It wasn't because of talent, opportunities, or status. It was because of their faith in God.

Please understand this. These people were not perfect. They weren't superheroes with mutant powers far beyond that of other mortals. In fact, they were far from it. They failed often, in small, petty ways and, in some cases, terrible and tragic ways. They didn't get their portraits hung in the Hall of Faith because they led such exemplary lives or had impressive résumés. They became heroes in the Hall of Faith because they had faith in a great God and simply acted on that faith. They were thermostats surrounded by thermometers. And we can be the same.

Dive in most anywhere in Hebrews 11 and you will see what I mean. Gideon, as we will see in an upcoming chapter, was a frightened, intimidated farmer when the angel of the Lord appeared to him with a commission from Heaven. He had been in hiding, terrorized by the cruel and powerful Midianites who had been oppressing the people of Israel. The Bible says that Gideon was trying to thresh wheat while hunkered down inside a winepress. I've never tried that myself, but it doesn't strike me as the stuff of legends.

According to Judges 6:12, "The Angel of the LORD appeared to him, and said to him, 'The LORD is with you, you mighty man of valor!'"

Gideon must have thought this was a case of mistaken identity. Surely God didn't look for heroes and champions crouching fearfully in dark places. We can imagine him looking up and saying, "Are you talking to me?" At that moment he didn't resemble a mighty man of valor even remotely. He was timid, afraid, and discouraged. But God didn't see Gideon for who he was in that moment. *God saw him for who he could become.* Gideon was a thermostat in the making.

A few verses further on in Hebrews 11, we bump into Moses. He was a fugitive from justice when the Lord spoke to him. Then came Jephthah—an illegitimate son unwanted by his family—who made some tragic life decisions that broke people's hearts, including his own.

These are very ordinary, run-of-the-mill people that God touched, but they responded by running the race set before them. Some of them ran it better than others. Some ran well from beginning to end. Others ran well, fell into the mud, but got up again and finished their race.

The people of Hebrews 11 are sinners just like you and me. And you know what's interesting about their accounts in Hebrews 11? You won't find one single mention of any of their sins in this chapter. If you go back and read the accounts of these folks, there were most certainly sins—and in some cases, very serious ones. Yet in Hebrews 11, this retrospective on their lives, there isn't a single mention of sin or humiliation or failure or disgrace.

Not one word of their many failures is mentioned in Hebrews 11. Why? Because they were forgiven and God gave them a second chance.

But there's an all-important aspect to each of these stories. We wouldn't even be reading about them if those individuals hadn't decided to climb, crawl, or lurch back into the race after some pretty spectacular failures. Some of the most consequential moments in all of life land at our feet in the aftermath of deep and humiliating personal catastrophes. If we deliberately turn to God in those moments, embarrassing and disappointing as they may be, if we choose to dive deep into the ocean of grace that's been made available to us, there will be more to our story. It may even end up being the best part.

That's the great good news. There can still be redemption. Even if you have been out of action for a long time, even if you are ninety-eight years old and in a nursing home, you can still get back on the course and finish your race. You might be hobbling, you might be in a wheelchair, you might even be crawling. But if these people could get back on course, so can you. Just because you started well and then made a mess of things doesn't mean you can't get up and head for that finish line. And when you do, you will accomplish it the same way the men and women in Hebrews 11 accomplished it. By faith.

Faith in Life's Gym

Faith is a lot like a muscle. The more you use a muscle—or the more you *break down* a muscle—the stronger the muscle becomes. If you neglect your muscles, they simply won't develop. If you neglect them for too long, they can even atrophy.

Not long ago I was at the gym and noticed a bodybuilder. I can't explain why, but this individual had evidently decided he only wanted to build his upper body. And he was doing a good job of it. He had massive arms, shoulders, chest, and classic six-pack abs. But when he was walking across the room, I couldn't help but notice that he had skinny chicken legs. I was thinking to myself, *Don't ever wear shorts, pal. It won't do you any favors.* It was like he had said, "I want to have a strong upper body, but I don't care about the rest."

That's how some Christians are. They have never set out to exercise their faith. As a result, they are underdeveloped—and not nearly as strong in the Lord as they could be. When they find themselves in a crisis where they really need a strong faith in the Lord, they falter.

Again, faith is like muscle. You have to use it or lose it. In the little New Testament book of Jude, we read these strong words: "But you, dear friends, carefully build yourselves up in this most holy faith by praying in the Holy Spirit, staying right at the center of God's love, keeping your arms open and outstretched, ready for the mercy of our Master, Jesus Christ. This is the unending life, the *real* life!" (vv. 20–21 MSG).

Notice that this Scripture is telling us that *faith does things.* Faith is active. The writer is saying, "Be praying. Be staying. Do things with your faith, and don't neglect it!"

For some reason I'm reminded of the people in Southern California who drive beautiful, gleaming four-wheel-drive vehicles on the freeway. I see them all over, often with a bunch of cool aftermarket accessories. Sometimes they raise these rigs and equip them with giant, gnarly tires, a huge winch on the front, and massive lights on top.

When one of these guys pulls up behind me on the street, I look in my rearview mirror and find myself staring at the chassis of their truck. But it's funny. I might ask one of them, "Hey, do you get out much with this? Do you do a lot of four-wheeling up in the hills?"

His reply is usually something like, "Are you kidding me? Do you know how much money I spent on this thing? There's no way I want to take it out in the dirt."

"So where are you going now?"

"I'm going to another car wash. The one with the tire gloss and super-triple-wax finish."

So all of that horsepower and potential and engineering never makes it off the freeways or surface streets. What a waste! You need to take that bad boy and use it for what it was designed for.

That's what faith is like for us sometimes. We talk about it, put it on the shelf, and dust it every now and then, but we're reluctant to use it. We treat faith like it is a fragile egg. When I find myself at the market on grocery duty, I may walk out of the store with ten grocery bags. But if I happen to drop one, it's always the one with the eggs. Never the cans! Who cares about a dented can? And never the bread. The bread can take it. It is always the eggs that end up in a premature omelet at the bottom of the bag.

Sometimes we treat our faith that way. *Be careful! Don't bump it. Don't breathe on it.* No! Take it out of the carton and use it. Get it dirty. Put it into action. Watch what God can do.

Faith Does Things

Let's dive in a little deeper now and see what Hebrews 11 has to say about faith and people of faith. We will start with the first ten verses.

> Now faith is the substance of things hoped for, the evidence of things not seen. For by it the elders obtained a good testimony.
>
> By faith we understand that the worlds were framed by the word of God, so that the things which are seen were not made of things which are visible.
>
> By faith Abel offered to God a more excellent sacrifice than Cain, through which he obtained witness that he was righteous, God testifying of his gifts; and through it he being dead still speaks.
>
> By faith Enoch was taken away so that he did not see death, "and was not found, because God had taken him"; for before he was taken he had this testimony, that he pleased God. But without faith it is impossible to please Him, for he who comes to God must believe that He is, and that He is a rewarder of those who diligently seek Him.

By faith Noah, being divinely warned of things not yet seen, moved with godly fear, prepared an ark for the saving of his household, by which he condemned the world and became heir of the righteousness which is according to faith.

By faith Abraham obeyed when he was called to go out to the place which he would receive as an inheritance. And he went out, not knowing where he was going. By faith he dwelt in the land of promise as in a foreign country, dwelling in tents with Isaac and Jacob, the heirs with him of the same promise; for he waited for the city which has foundations, whose builder and maker is God.

So many verses here speak of how faith *worked*. Abel offered a sacrifice. Noah got out his carpentry tools and prepared an ark. Abraham obeyed and later even offered up Isaac.

It comes down to this. A faith with no works is a faith that does not work. These people in the Hall of Faith—stumbling and fumbling as they may have been at times—actually *used* their faith. It's a simple reality of life that you can't run and stand still at the same time. If you are sitting, you are not running; if you are running, you are not sitting. How we all wish we could find some La-Z-Boy that we could recline in and still get all the benefits of exercise. But there is no such thing. In the same way, if we are running in the race of life, we can't stay still. Faith is getting out on the track and pushing the pace.

We tell people in crisis, "Just have faith. Trust in God. Believe in the Lord, and He will get you through." And that's all well and good until we find a crisis on our own doorstep. We get a letter in the mail, a phone call in the night, or a scary word from the doctor, and suddenly all that sage counsel about faith seems like just words to us.

I heard an anecdote about a woman who had a crazy husband. She went to her pastor and said, "Pastor, my husband tells me that if I keep coming to the church, he'll kill me."

"Now, now," the pastor soothed her. "Don't be afraid. Have faith in God. The Lord will protect you."

A week later she came back again, even more frightened. "Pastor, he's said it again! He told me right out that if I keep coming to this church, he'll really *kill* me. I think he means it!"

"Just trust in the Lord. Do the right thing. The Lord will protect you."

She came back several more times, sharing this same fear and worry with the pastor. Each time he patiently reminded her to have faith in the Lord. Then one day she came into his office and said, "Pastor, my husband just said if I keep coming to this church, he's going to kill *you*."

The pastor replied, "You ought to look into that church on the other side of town that just started up. I've heard good things. It would be a good place for you to land."

In other words, it's easy to tell others to have faith until you find your own feet in the fire and find your own faith tested.

Faith Grows Stronger through Testing

As I noted, muscles get stronger from being broken down and then built up. And the same is true of faith. I like the way the J. B. Phillips translation of the Bible captures the words of James 1:2–3: "When all kinds of trials and temptations crowd into your lives my brothers, don't resent them as intruders, but welcome them as friends! Realise that they come to test your faith and to produce in you the quality of endurance."

God will test your faith for your own good.

I know you would like to have a trouble-free life. So would I. I know you would like to have a temptation-free life. Me too. But since the fall of man in Genesis 3, that has never been in the cards. Jesus Himself told us, "Here on earth you will have many trials and sorrows" (John 16:33 NLT).

It has been said that one Christian who has been tempted is worth a thousand who haven't been. I'm sure you've also heard Christians compared to tea bags. You don't know what they are like or what they have in them until after they're put in really hot water.

Maybe you are in hot water right now. The hot water of temptation. The hot water of difficulty. Your faith is being tested. Know this: God won't give you more than you can handle, but you can handle more than you think. If the Lord gave it to you, you can handle it. If you couldn't handle it, He wouldn't have given it to you. He will give you only what you are ready for.

Think of Abraham. The Lord started by telling him to leave his country. Later on, He told Abraham to take his only son and lay him on the altar. He started with one test and that led to another, even harder test.

Jesus once told Peter to move his boat into deeper waters. Later on, He told Peter to walk on water. The point is, He didn't go for the hard thing in the beginning. He let Peter build up to it. You are going through a series of tests in your Christian life and each one will make you stronger. Everything you experience is preparation for something else.

Sometimes we wimp out and cry to God that we can't handle it. The prophet Jeremiah came to a place in his life where he wanted to drop out of the race, complaining to the Lord that he was in over his head and couldn't take it anymore. The Lord's response, in Jeremiah 12:5, was classic.

> So, Jeremiah, if you're worn out in this footrace
>   with men,
> what makes you think you can race against horses?
> And if you can't keep your wits during times of
>   calm,
> what's going to happen when troubles break loose
>   like the Jordan in flood? (MSG)

In other words, "Man, toughen up! If you want to run with the horses, don't get worried when you are in a footrace with mere men. If you don't trust me with your life now, what will happen when the really big trials come?"

By the way, if you want to be a world changer, hang around with other world changers. Spend time with people who want to have faith, want to trust God, and try hard to obey Him. If you're always rubbing shoulders with people who let the world change them, it can drag you down. If you want to run with the horses, don't hang around with the donkeys. That was what God was saying to Jeremiah. "It's time to step up your game."

Faith may involve our emotions at times, but faith is not a feeling. Faith is obeying God in spite of feelings, circumstances, consequences, or opposition. That's what the people in Hebrews 11 did, and that's what made such an indelible impact on their world.

What Is Faith?

Can anyone really define faith?

Hebrews 11:1 sets out to do just that. We read, "Faith is the substance of things hoped for, the evidence of things not seen." The New Living Translation puts it this way: "Faith shows the reality of what we hope for; it is the evidence of things we cannot see."

It comes down to this. Faith is believing in invisible things. It sees what could be, with God in the equation. The following quote has been attributed to the great missionary statesman Oswald Sanders: "Faith enables the believing soul to treat the future as present and the invisible as seen."

Remember when Jesus tested His disciple Philip? A huge crowd was pressing in on Jesus and His men from all directions, and Jesus knew they would be hungry and want some lunch. Turning to Philip, Jesus asked, "Where can we buy bread to feed all these people?" Scripture tells us that Jesus was testing His disciple and already knew how He would handle the situation.

Philip, however, had no idea what the Lord had in mind, and was freaking out. He replied, "Even if we worked for months, we wouldn't have enough money to feed them!" (John 6:7 NLT).

What Jesus wanted Philip to say was, "I have no idea how we could do such a thing. Seems impossible to me. But if You are part of the equation, Lord, we can get it done somehow."

You and I can look at our world and see huge, seemingly impossible problems in front of us. But with faith we can see solutions because we have an all-wise, all-powerful God who can accomplish *anything.*

Look at the state of America right now, with all its problems, divisions, and moral breakdown. Sometimes it's enough to make me want to wring my hands and say, "Oh no, oh no, I don't know what's going to happen. I don't know what to do." But wait a second. When I look at this country through the eyes of faith, I say to myself, "God could change this. God could send a mighty spiritual awakening to our land." And I start praying for that.

Maybe you have a marriage that's coming apart at the seams. You've tried this and you've tried that, and nothing seems to work. In fact, the problems are only getting worse. You say, "It's over! I can't turn this around. There's nothing I can do."

Maybe not. But there *is* something God can do. Maybe it's time to bring faith into the equation and take some action. A humble, from-the-heart apology is often a great place to start.

Faith Takes Action

Faith doesn't just talk about action. Faith doesn't live in the realm of theory. Faith doesn't live on Facebook posts or greeting cards with pretty pictures and nice words in fancy calligraphy.

Faith is not found in flowery posts of sunsets on Instagram or Pinterest. Faith lives in the real world, the world of activity. It rolls up its sleeves and *does* things. Picture a non-Christian friend or family member in your mind, someone you couldn't imagine turning to the Lord in a hundred years. If you try to imagine that individual holding a Bible or talking about Jesus, the picture seems almost laughable. It could never happen.

But that's not true. It could happen. Nobody but *nobody* in the first century would have laid odds on the close-minded

Christian-killer named Saul of Tarsus becoming a missionary and a tenderhearted church planter. But that's what happened. God can convert anyone. God can transform any heart. Do you believe that? Then act on it. Start praying for that person in your life. Invite them to church. Invite them to a Christian concert or evangelistic crusade.

"It's no good," you say. "You don't know this person. They will say no so fast it will make your head spin."

All right . . . but what if they don't? What if they say yes? How will you ever know if you don't try?

"But I don't want to try and fail," you say. "I don't want to be rejected."

Why not? I would rather try and fail than not try at all, wouldn't you? That is faith. Faith takes risks. Faith will bet the farm on something. Faith will say, "Let's just see what the Lord will do." But if you sit around in your safe zone and never venture out, trusting in the Lord, you can be very sure of the result.

Nothing will happen at all.

Faith Can Make the Difference

Faith can make the difference between something happening or not happening, between receiving or not receiving what God has for us.

One time when Jesus and His disciples had ventured north of Samaria, near the cities of Tyre and Sidon, a Gentile woman came to him with a young daughter in deep trouble who needed supernatural help. She pleaded with Jesus to intervene, believing that His intervention would make all the difference.

And it did. Jesus said, "Woman, great is your faith! Let it be to you as you desire" (Matt. 15:28).

It's interesting that in Nazareth, in the Lord's own hometown where He grew up, He didn't do many miracles because of the people's unbelief. Jesus had begun His public ministry and was becoming widely known across the land. But back in Nazareth, people were saying, "Are you kidding me? Jesus? We knew His mom and dad. We've known Jesus since He was a kid. He used to play in the streets here. He helped out in His dad's carpenter shop. Now people are saying He might be the Messiah? No way. We won't believe that."

Because of that mindset, guess what?

"He did not do many mighty works there because of their unbelief" (Matt. 13:58).

No faith means no mighty works. But faith—even faith the size of a tiny mustard seed—opens the door to mighty, mind-blowing, supernatural works right in the middle of your situation, no matter how messy it might be.

People will sometimes say, "That sounds nice, but those things could never happen to me. God would never do that for me." And the sad thing is, they are probably right. But if they began to seek the Lord with all their heart, asking for the impossible and believing in the power and love of God to grant it, their situation might be completely different.

There is another story in the gospels that moves me each time I read it. It's the account of a woman with a debilitating medical condition that was robbing her of strength and dignity.[1] In desperation, she had spent all her money on quack doctors, but it was to no avail. When someone told her Jesus was passing through her town, it started a train of thought in her mind. She must have told herself, "If I could just work my way through the crowd somehow and touch Him. No—if I could just touch the edge of His robe as He passes by, I could be healed! I have to try!"

And that's what she did. She took a risk, wormed her way through the packed masses of people (probably frowning at her and giving her dirty looks), reached out, and let the tips of her trembling fingers just barely graze the fabric of His robe. Jesus hadn't laid a hand on her or spoken a single word to her. But power flowed from Him like summer lightning, and she knew in an instant that she was healed.

Jesus stopped in His tracks and said, "Who touched Me?" His disciples said, "Lord, everyone is touching You. Everyone is shoving and jostling and tugging at You. What do you mean, 'Who touched Me?'" But Jesus knew that someone had touched Him in faith.

At that, the crowd parted and the frightened woman came forward, fell on her knees before Him, and admitted that she had been the one. Did He rebuke her? No, He commended her.

"Daughter, you took a risk trusting me, and now you're healed and whole. Live well, live blessed!" (Luke 8:48 MSG).

What did this woman do? She left her house, her endless misery, and her depression and plunged into the crowd. She got up and moved. She reached out and put her faith into action. We need to do the same. If you don't reach out to God, not much will happen. In fact, Hebrews 11:6 reminds us: "Without faith it is impossible to please Him, for he who comes to God must believe that He is, and that He is a rewarder of those who diligently seek Him."

If this book is about world changers, who is the first one we encounter in Hebrews 11?

As a matter of fact, it is *you.*

You say, "What do you mean, me? My name isn't in there."

Actually, in a way it is. There is a place you can insert yourself into the text of the Hall of Faith chapter. Look at verse 3 of Hebrews 11 again. "By faith we understand that the worlds were framed by the word of God, so that the things which are seen were not made of things which are visible."

Who is the "we" in this verse?

It's us. It's you and me. "By faith *we* understand." The first space for a world changer, for this incredible, enduring roster of faithful saints, is inclusive, and you are invited to add your name. Faith is not elitist. It's not only for saints enshrined in stained glass or people on pedestals. It is for all of us.

When we talk about faith, we're not talking about some random power in the universe that anyone with determination can tap into. Many fairy tales and Disney movies promote the idea of wishing upon a star or believing in yourself in order to make your dreams come true. Some might translate this to: "Just have faith and life will get better."

No, it won't. Faith in nothing produces nothing. I'm not talking about having faith in faith here; I'm talking about having faith in God. Again, in verse 3 we read, "By faith we understand that the worlds were framed by the word of God." So the object of our faith is God Almighty. As we've been told, it's important to put our faith in Him.

We All Live by Faith

Some people, possibly some people you know very well, say things like, "I don't believe in faith. I am a person who believes in facts, not fiction. I believe you must see something to believe in it. Faith is for fools."

I have had people like this in my life too. And my reply to them goes something like this: "Seriously? Come on. You use faith all the time. What about the last time you walked into a restaurant and ordered a meal? That server was probably a complete stranger to you. And how do you know what *really* happened behind those doors in the kitchen? You don't know how that food was stored or prepared and handled. You don't know if the employees followed safety standards or health standards or prepared your meal properly. In light of the COVID-19 crisis, you can't confirm that they washed their hands regularly and maintained proper social distancing requirements. And yet when the server set the food down in front of you on the table, you picked up your fork and started putting the food into your mouth! Really? Don't you think that takes a little faith?

"Or how about when you went to that doctor for a diagnosis? The doctor told you that you needed surgery, so you scheduled it with the surgery center or hospital, reported in, and let them stick a needle in your vein. You let yourself be put to sleep while some strangers opened you up and did things in your body. You let them do that. You had faith in the diagnosis. You had faith in the hospital and the surgeon and the anesthesiologist.

"And then there was that time you got on board a Boeing 747 and buckled yourself in. Though you know very little about aerodynamics, you trusted that somehow—even though the jet has a takeoff weight of 900,000 pounds—this monstrosity of metal loaded to the gills with explosive fuel would get you into the air and deliver you to your destination. You were also applying faith toward the people in the cockpit, that they didn't get their pilots' licenses online from a site called 'Pilots 'R Us!'

"Don't tell me you don't use faith. You use faith every day. You put your faith in pilots and doctors and servers and chefs and pharmacists. And God is saying, 'Put your faith in Me, the One who created the stars and planets and gave you a beating heart and breath in your lungs. The One who sent His Son to save you from sin and give you eternal life so that you could live forever with Him in Heaven.'"

Every one of us will end up putting our faith in something.

You might as well have faith in the Faithful One, who has promised to never leave or forsake you.

The World Changer Who Was Out of This World

It was by faith that Enoch was taken up to heaven without dying—"he disappeared, because God took him." For before he was taken up, he was known as a person who pleased God.

~Hebrews 11:5 NLT

When I was in high school, I went out for track and field and actually did pretty well. I liked sprints the best, because the pain was limited to a shorter time frame. I could push on the gas all the way to the floorboard, run my hardest, and then it was over, and I could go sit in the shade.

The older I got, however, the less I liked running, and eventually I traded it in for walking. That's where I've been ever since. I could be completely content with walking if someone I know wasn't pushing me a little to pick up the pace.

Often my wife and I will walk together. Sometimes she will say to me, "Come on, Greg. Let's just run to the end of the block."

"No, no thank you," I will say. "I like to walk."

I know her tricks. If I agree to run to the end of the block with her, she will say, "Let's go one more block. We can do it!"

Her motives, I'm sure, are the best. She is trying to get me to be more active, maybe thinking it will help me to live longer. But I am content to just keep on walking right into eternity.

At the end of the walk, I'm ready to kick back and relax a little. But not Cathe. She will tell me, "I'm going to go meet some of my girlfriends and go for another walk." I may not see her again for hours. Why? Because when she takes walks with her friends, it's different than when guys take walks. I tell her, "Why don't you just call it what it is? When you go out with the girls, it's not a walk, it's a *talk*."

She knows I'm teasing, because the walk-talk these women experience is a good thing in many ways. Women and girls love to communicate. I have made this amazing discovery. Women seem to enjoy talking in general more than men do. Have you noticed that too?

I think women have it right in using their walks as opportunities for friendship and communication, because when the Bible speaks of *walking with God* that is exactly what it should be. It's not just a walk, it's a talk. It is all about communication.

When you make the promise to walk through life with someone, you are basically saying that you will be there with that person through the highs and lows, through the rough patches and the mountaintop moments. You are there to love them and to understand them. When we say we are "walking with God," it's essentially the same. But even more.

In this chapter we will talk about a somewhat mysterious man named Enoch from way, way back near the beginning of everything. He was a man who walked with God (please note that he didn't sprint) and ended up walking right into Heaven without dying. We weren't there, of course, but I can almost imagine what happened. After taking many enjoyable walks together and getting deeper and deeper into conversation through the years, it's almost as if the Lord turned to Enoch and said, "Hey buddy, we've walked a long way, and we're closer to My house than we are to yours. Why don't you just come on home with Me?"

Enoch was a world changer and one of the first names inscribed in the Hall of Faith in Hebrews 11. How did he change his world? It's worth our while to dive deeper into his story and find out.

Waiting for Change?

John Mayer has a song called "Waiting on the World to Change." The lyrics to the chorus repeat the title phrase over and over.

Whenever I hear that song, I find myself thinking, *Good luck with that, John. You'll be waiting a long time, because this world isn't going to change.*

Changing your world begins with you, and it begins with faith in a great and powerful God who will use you as a change agent if you let Him. When you step out in faith, God will work through your obedience. But if you don't step out in faith, you can't really expect much to happen. God works through people who apply their faith.

One of the themes of Hebrews 11 and 12 is running the race of life, and that's a compelling word picture. But faith isn't just running the race, it is also walking the walk. It is following Him hour by hour and day by day. Hebrews 10:38 says, "The just shall *live* by faith" (emphasis added). Feelings come and go. You can't attach your Christian experience to how you are feeling emotionally in the moment. You must learn how to walk by faith.

I have discovered a big secret of a successful Christian life. Are you ready for it? It is living and walking by faith each and every day. You might not think that's very profound, or you might say, "I've heard all that before." That may be. But it bears repeating. In reality it's the most important thing you will ever do. Author Eugene Peterson called this walk of faith "a long obedience in the same direction." It is following Christ with consistency. It is staying with it. That is the kind of person who is going to change the world.

And that brings us to Enoch.

The Longest Walk

My wife takes really long walks with her girlfriends, but Enoch walked with God for over three hundred years. Think of it. If Enoch ever had a midlife crisis, it would have been at around age one hundred and fifty. People lived longer back in those early days on earth before the full effects of human-kind's sin had kicked in.

When it comes to studying the life of Enoch, there really isn't much to go on. We first encounter him in the book of Genesis, where Scripture says: "When Enoch was 65 years old, he became the father of Methuselah. After the birth of Methuselah, Enoch lived in close fellowship with God for another 300 years, and he had other sons and daughters. Enoch lived 365 years, walking in close fellowship with God. Then one day he disappeared, because God took him" (5:21–24 NLT).

When did Enoch walk with God? It was a long, long time ago. But I might add that it was during one of the darkest times in human history. We really can't imagine how dark it was. In fact, it was so warped, perverted, and evil that God actually said, "I am sorry that I even made man in the first place." God was about to bring judgment on earth through the great flood.

Enoch, however, lived in the time before that flood. In a sense, he was a last days believer—only these were the last days before the worldwide deluge that swept away everyone but Noah and his family. We, too, are last days believers, waiting for the judgment of God to come. But even more we are waiting for the return of Christ when He will catch us up in the air to meet Him in the clouds (see 1 Thess. 4:13–18).

Why do I bring this up? Because Jesus told us that "as it was in the days of Noah, so it will be at the coming of the Son of Man" (Matt. 24:37 NIV). In other words, these are parallel universes. The time we are living in right now in some ways mirrors the time before God judged the world with the great flood. They are similar times, with similar hazards and dangers. And if Enoch was able to live a godly life at a time like this, if he was able to maintain a consistent walk with God, then you and I can live a godly life wherever we are right now.

Enoch walked with God in an ungodly world until the day God took him home. But this isn't just ancient history. It can be our story too. The same spiritual resources that were available to Enoch are available to us. We can live godly lives in an ungodly world. You might say, "Greg, I've got a situation going in my life that you don't understand. You don't know my world. You don't know my family. You don't know what it's like to live in my neighborhood. You don't know what my workplace is like, or what it's like to live on my campus."

Maybe I don't. But I do know this. No matter how messed up or evil your environment might be, you can live for Jesus Christ in an ungodly world, and Enoch proves it.

Enoch Walked with God

As I mentioned earlier, the Bible doesn't say that Enoch sprinted with God. Some Christians go through periods in their lives when they experience a burst of energy and a surge of great passion for the Lord. Then, down the road somewhere, they collapse in a heap. Or maybe they walk away altogether, which makes us wonder if they were ever really Christians to begin with.

Enoch *walked* with God. To walk implies making progress; you're getting somewhere. He was further along at one hundred than he was at sixty-five. He was further along at two hundred and fifty than he was at one hundred and ninety-nine.

Here's what all of us need to remember. Spiritual growth doesn't happen overnight. It takes time, it takes perseverance, and it takes step after step after step. In 1 John 1:7, we read: "If we walk in the light as He is in the light, we have fellowship with one another, and the blood of Jesus Christ His Son cleanses us from all sin." Romans 13:13 says: "Let us walk properly, as in the day, not in revelry and drunkenness, not in lewdness and lust, not in strife and envy."

God is saying, "If you are a Christian, act like a Christian. Walk like a Christian. Behave like a Christian. Don't get caught up in wild parties and immorality or selfish preoccupations."

Notice the verse from Romans also mentions "strife and envy" or as another translation puts it, "dissension and jealousy" (NIV).

We might pride ourselves on the fact that we don't get drunk or sleep around, and don't get me wrong, avoiding those things is essential for a true follower of Jesus Christ. But do you argue and quarrel with people? Are you a jealous person? Those sins are mentioned as well. In 1 John 2:6, it says, "He who says he abides in Him ought himself also to walk just as He walked." The apostle Paul agrees, writing, "But I say, walk by the Spirit, and you will not carry out the desire of the flesh" (Gal. 5:16 NASB).

What does it mean specifically and practically to walk with God?

There is a verse in the Old Testament that addresses this truth in a beautiful way, telling us what it really means to walk with God as Enoch did. Very simply, Amos 3:3 says, "Can two walk together, unless they are agreed?"

It's a short verse but it's loaded with meaning. Right off the top we can identify three solid truths that show us how to walk with the living God.

Walk Together as a Unit

When the verse speaks of two walking together, it means doing so as a single unit. In the Message translation, Amos 3:3 reads: "Do two people walk hand in hand if they aren't going to the same place?" In other words, walking with God is *getting in sync* with God.

We could compare it to riding a tandem bicycle. Have you ever ridden one of those? One person on the front and the other on the back. Let's imagine that I was out for a ride through our neighborhood with my wife. She is up front, pedaling for all she is worth, and I am in back tapping on the brakes. Am I being helpful? No. For that tandem thing to work we have to pedal together. We have to find a rhythm. That is what it means to walk with God.

We might also use music to illustrate this. I don't know about you, but wherever I go I hear music. I don't just mean audibly. I *notice* music. I recognize tunes. I take note of what song is playing.

Cathe and I might be in an elevator and I will suddenly say, "Hey, they're playing 'The Lion Sleeps Tonight.'"

"What? What are you talking about?"

"The music. I remember that song from when I was a kid."

"You're listening to music in an elevator? I didn't even notice it."

If I'm in a restaurant and a familiar song comes over the sound system, I will start singing along—which might make the other people at the table stare at me. (I can handle it.) I also notice when singers go off pitch. I know pitch, and when someone gets off, I cringe just a little.

Here is what we need to understand. God is always on pitch.

Leonard Bernstein, the celebrated orchestra conductor, was once asked, "What is the hardest instrument to play?" He replied, "Second fiddle. I can always find plenty of first violinists, but to find someone who plays second violin with as much enthusiasm, that's a problem."[1]

We need to understand that God is first violinist; we are second fiddle. God is the lead singer, and we are the backup vocalists. Or maybe God is the lead guitar, and we're the drums or rhythm. If we're not following along with Him, if we're not tracking with His lead, we're going to get off-key and out of sync with Him. We won't be making beautiful music together, and the fault will lie with us.

Why do I bring this up? Because sometimes you and I might say we want to walk with God when the truth is we want Him to walk with us, to follow our lead. *Come on, God. Here's where we're going. Here's the pace I want. Here are the stops I want to make.*

Of course, that can never be. God won't submit to our direction, our timing, or our agenda. No, if I want to walk with God, I have to let Him lead. I have to let Him set the pace. I have to match my stride to His and harmonize with Him.

This may seem too obvious or basic to you. But in reality it's something Christians wrestle with every day of their lives. He is God and you are not. You are in a support role, not a lead. This isn't about *you*, this is about God and His plans for your life. To walk with God means two people walking together as a single unit. It is understanding that when you do this, when you live this way, your Christian life will start firing on all cylinders.

That's what Enoch did as he walked with God in a world that was teetering on the knife edge of judgment and destruction. Some of the paths Enoch and God walked along might have been dark, with twists and turns and obstacles along the way. But they always walked together. God set the pace and Enoch kept up for over three centuries, neither running ahead nor lagging behind. And then one day they turned a corner and Enoch followed God right through a gate and into Heaven.

Let me quote 1 John 2:6 again: "He who says he abides in Him ought himself also to walk just as He walked." In actuality, the terms *walking* and *abiding* are interchangeable metaphors. Yes, I know that one implies motion and the other means staying put, but the concept is the same. It all boils down to staying in fellowship with Jesus. The Lord says to us, "If you want to walk with Me, you need to abide in Me." In John 15:7, Jesus said, "If you abide in Me, and My words abide in you, you will ask what you desire, and it shall be done for you."

When I am in sync with God, I will start praying according to His will. I will be in harmony with Him. As a result, I will start seeing a lot more of my prayers answered in the affirmative.

Years ago I was scuba diving in Hawaii. I am a certified scuba diver, but I am pretty rusty at it right now since I rarely dive anymore. If I do dive, it won't be any farther than ten or twenty feet. On this occasion, however, I was doing what was for me a really deep dive, over one hundred feet, off the island of Molokini. I will be honest with you. When I got all the equipment on—mask, snorkel, regulator, tanks, inflatable vest, weight belt, fins, and so on—I had a weird anxiety attack.

Suddenly, I didn't want to go down. Then I remembered that I'd already paid for the dive. If I didn't go, I'd just be sitting in the boat eating everyone's sandwiches while they explored the ocean. Besides that, I knew they would make fun of me afterwards.

So I told myself, *Greg, you are going to do this. You are going down.*

And I went down.

Right from the start, however, I was anxious and nervous. A friend told me later that he noticed me breathing like crazy, with lots of bubbles. Finally I got to the bottom, a hundred feet down. When you're that far underwater, you can't just shoot to the surface or your lungs will expand beyond capacity and explode. You have to be very careful.

When I glanced at my air gauge, I saw that it was almost on empty. Immediately, I looked around for the instructor, making the universal sign for "I am out of air! I'm going to die!" I still remember the moment. Even through his mask I saw our diving coach roll his eyes. He was probably thinking, *What an idiot.* He gestured me to come over to him and pointed to the tanks on his back. He had two tanks, and the rest of us had one. Through his gestures, I understood that he wanted me to breathe off this extra regulator.

Quickly, fearing that my next breath would be my last, I pulled out my regulator and grabbed his extra. *Ahh, I'm breathing. Breathing is good. I love breathing. I'm good to go now.*

But there was a problem. I was now attached to the instructor and had to go wherever he wanted to go. Not only that, my hose was really short, meaning I had to do short, shallow strokes to stay in proximity to him. Where he moved, I moved, doing my best to hover above him.

It was a little humiliating, to tell you the truth. I couldn't go where I wanted to go anymore or do my own thing. I was attached to the instructor's air regulator and had to stay in sync with him.

Following him was life, going my own way meant death.

That's the best illustration I can think of to show how Enoch stayed true to God for three hundred years in a very dark time in very challenging circumstances. He walked with God. He moved with God. And he stayed in sync.

That's what we need to do in the challenges of our lives as well.

Keep Your Appointments with God

Have you ever been late for an appointment? Worse still, are you chronically late? The problem with late people is that they don't know they are late people. Here is how to determine if you are a late person. You text me, "I am five minutes away" when you are really sitting on your couch in your sweats. Or your friends tell you to get there at 8:00 a.m. but they tell everyone else to arrive at 8:30, because they know you won't show up on time.

Here is another way to determine whether you are a late person. When you actually arrive on time for a meeting someone looks at you and says, "What are you doing here?" I know you have many good and logical reasons for being late. But when it becomes a pattern and you are always late, always running fifteen to thirty minutes behind schedule, let me be a little blunt with you. It's kind of rude. It's especially rude if you are meeting me for a meal somewhere and I am hungry and my wife won't let me order until you get there.

I will say, "Cathe, let's order an appetizer."

And she'll say, "No, Greg, that's rude. We need to wait." And then when you finally do arrive, I'm not in my normal good mood.

My friend Bob Shank has a saying that I subscribe to. "Early is on time. On time is late. Late is never acceptable."

It is one thing to be late for an appointment with a friend.

It is another thing to be late for an appointment with God.

If you belong to God, He has an appointment with you. You might say, "I didn't see that on my calendar." Maybe not, but the appointment is there. Every day. You need to make time for the Lord. That's what it means to walk with God.

Personally, I find mornings the best time to spend with God. I admit that I have to have coffee first, because I want to be in my right mind before I have an audience with the King. But after half a cup of a fresh brew, I get into the Word and spend a little time in prayer, committing my day to the Lord.

You may be thinking, "But Greg, you don't know my schedule. I have so much to do. I have to update my Facebook page. I have to log on to Twitter and check Instagram."

The latest research tells us that American adults say they open a social media app on their phone at least ten times a day.[2] That's basically once every waking hour. For teenagers, that number may be one hundred times a day![3] What would happen if all the time Christians devote to Twitter and Facebook was invested in prayer for Christ to transform our culture?

We all have stuff we want to do and like to do and have to do. But we need to keep our appointments with God. *How can two walk together unless they are agreed?* Maybe you think it was easier for Enoch because he didn't have all the modern distractions that we do. But I don't think that will wash. Enoch lived in an era that was tiptoeing on the edge of the abyss; the times were unhappy, violent, and dangerous. Besides that, when you live to be three hundred, you can't even count how many kids, grandkids, great-grandkids, and great-great-grandkids you have. Think of all the ballet recitals and soccer games he would have been expected to attend. Somehow, he kept his walk with God number one.

Adam used to have an appointment with God every day in the garden of Eden. It was an appointment that even predated Eve. Just imagine this. The Lord would show up every day when the sun was setting to take a little stroll around the garden with His friend Adam. I don't know if God took on human form or if He spoke audibly. Genesis 3:8 says that Adam "heard the sound" of the Lord approaching. What was that? The gravel crunching under sandaled feet? A sweet, cool breath of wind that stirred the palm fronds? The Bible doesn't say. We don't even know if the Lord spoke with an audible voice. But we do know this. They had some wonderful, indescribable fellowship together.

Then one day God showed up and Adam was late for his appointment. Why? Because Adam had sinned and was hiding from the Lord. And he heard God's voice calling, "Adam, where are you?"

I wonder if the Lord says that to some of us sometimes. "Where are you? How come I don't hear from you? How come you aren't reading My Word? How come you're not showing up at church with My people to worship Me? How come you're not praying? What's going on? I miss our times together. Where are you?"

Walking with God means keeping your appointments with Him.

To Walk with God Is to Pool Your Resources

That's another possible reading of Amos 3:3: "Can two walk together unless they pool their resources?"

Have you ever seen the TV show *Shark Tank*? Inventors and entrepreneurs try to convince successful businesspeople to invest in their products. The show can be quite entertaining when you see all the weird and wacky things people want these folks to invest their money in.

One guy came up with something he called a "man candle." (I'm not making this up.) Instead of having a fragrance of lilacs or lavender or whatever, these candles were supposed to smell like traditional things men like. One smelled like barbecue. Another smelled like an old football. Another smelled like a golf course—whatever that would be.

The idea was rejected. Men really don't want barbecue candles when they can go out back, light up the grill, and smell the real thing.

Another person came to the Shark Tank with a bird feeder that would prevent squirrels from stealing all the birdseed. The problem was that its deterrent was an electric jolt, but it couldn't really distinguish between squirrels and little birds. It zapped both of them.

Sometimes the ideas on *Shark Tank* do meet with success. One lady came up with what she called a Scrub Daddy. It's a sponge with a smiley face that turns soft in warm water and firm in cold. Since its introduction it has brought in more than one hundred million dollars in sales.

Here is how it works on the spiritual level. We come to God with our problems, our fears, our concerns, and our broken lives. We humbly say to Him, "Lord, I want to go into business with You." To be more accurate, He invites us into this relationship, and says, "Let's form a partnership. I want you to bring all your resources to the table. And I will bring all of Mine."

It's kind of ridiculous, isn't it? What do you and I bring to the table? It would be like going into business with Bill Gates as equal partners.

Bill Gates says to you, "What do you have to put on the table?"

"Well, I've been saving these pennies. I've got one hundred of them."

"Okay, you've got a buck. Put it on the table. What else do you have?"

"Umm, well, I've got some debts."

"Okay, what else?"

"Well, I do have some personal issues and problems. Quite a few of them, to be honest."

"What else?"

"That's about it, I'm afraid. But here it is. What do you have, Mr. Gates?"

"Billions and billions of dollars. In fact, I may be worth a billion more than I was an hour ago. I need to check. But that's what I bring to the table."

So there we are, in partnership with the living God who created the universe. We come with our problems and our weaknesses. We also come with our talents, our abilities, our dreams, and our aspirations. We come with all we are and all we have and lay it on the table. Then God comes to the table, the One who has all power in Heaven and earth, and He says, "I want to change you and transform you." What a deal.

What does it mean to walk with God? It means that you are in harmony with Him, you keep pace with Him, and that you are in business with Him.

What Does It Mean to Please God?

Enoch walked with God on all those levels, and you and I can too. In Hebrews 11:5, we read that "before he was taken he had this testimony, that he pleased God." Every Christian has a testimony. And what is that? It's your reputation. Enoch had a reputation among his family, friends, acquaintances, and enemies that he pleased God. Everyone knew that it was the most important thing in the world to him.

Your reputation is what people say about you. What are you known for? What kind of testimony do you have? Enoch pleased God, and that is an awesome testimony. May it be said of you and me that deep down, at the core of who we are, we are all about pleasing the Lord.

When you think about it, there are three people you can live to please in life. You can live to please yourself. If you do that, I can tell you right now that you will end up in a very narrow place, miserable and lonely. You might also try to live to please others. But that will always be frustrating because no matter how hard you try, you can't always please everyone—and you may end up pleasing no one at all. Finally, you can live to please God. That's what Enoch did, and that is what Jesus did. In John 8:29, He said, "The Father has not left Me alone, for I always do those things that please Him."

What a statement. I can't say that about myself. I wish I could. I don't always do the things that please God, but He has put a desire in my heart to move in that direction. It's what walking with Him is all about.

Before we wrap up this chapter, let me offer three quick points on what the Bible specifically says about pleasing God. If you want to live a life that pleases Him, and if you want that to be your reputation, here are a few tips.

When You Are Treated Unfairly, You Hang in There

First Peter 2:19–20 tells us: "*God is pleased with you* when you do what you know is right and patiently endure unfair treatment. Of course, you get no credit for being patient if you are beaten for doing wrong. But if you suffer for doing good and endure it patiently, God is pleased with you" (NLT, emphasis added).

Have you ever been mistreated, misunderstood, or unappreciated? Has anyone ever told a really hurtful lie about you and you wanted to get them back? The Bible says that if you patiently endure those trials and go on your way with a positive attitude, continuing to do what you know to be right, you will please the heart of God (who sees everything and misses nothing).

In the dark days before the flood covered the earth, Enoch was most certainly mocked, persecuted, excluded, and hassled for making the Lord his priority. But he kept right on walking with God.

Worship Him and Help Others

Hebrews 13:15–16 says, "Through Jesus, therefore, let us continually offer to God a sacrifice of praise—the fruit of lips that openly profess his name. And do not forget to do good and to share with others, *for with such sacrifices God is pleased*" (NIV, emphasis added).

When you worship the Lord—in fellowship with other believers or all by yourself—singing out loud and lifting your hands to praise His name, that pleases Him. It doesn't matter even a little if your pitch is off or if you get the words wrong. Sometimes we don't feel like praising the Lord, do we? We go to church, fold our arms, and say, "I don't want to praise God." "I didn't sleep well last night." "I've got a cold." "I just had a disagreement with my spouse." "My kids are driving me crazy." "I don't really feel like worshiping right now."

That is when you can offer the *sacrifice* of praise. You don't offer praise to God because you feel good, you offer praise to God because *He is good*. The Bible says, "Oh, give thanks to the LORD, for He is good! For His mercy endures forever" (Ps. 106:1).

The second part of Hebrews 13:15 speaks about helping someone in need.

It's when we say to someone, "Let me help you."

It's such a simple thing, but it's so powerful. *Let me get that door for you. . . . You seem troubled. Can I pray for you? . . . Do you need a ride? . . . Can we bring you a meal?* You don't have to think a lot about it or make it a big production. You just do it. You step into someone's life where there is a need and you help them out, as best you can. That pleases God. God likes it when we do those things.

I think we can conclude that Enoch didn't walk with God for three hundred years with his eyes locked skyward toward Heaven, ignoring the needs around him. He pleased God by pitching in and helping others whenever he had the chance.

Giving of Your Finances Is Pleasing to God

In Philippians 4:17–18, Paul says, "Not that I desire your gifts; what I desire is that more be credited to your account. I have received full payment and have more than enough. I am amply supplied, now that I have received from Epaphroditus the gifts you sent. They are a fragrant offering, an acceptable sacrifice, *pleasing to God*" (NIV, emphasis added).

When you give your finances to the Lord, He takes note, and it pleases Him. It's interesting that in this passage Paul seems to be saying, "I don't want you to do this for me. I want it to be credited to your eternal account in Heaven."

What do you think it means in Matthew 6:20 when Jesus said, "Lay up for yourselves treasures in heaven"? Does that imply that there's a pile of stuff waiting on the other side? No, but it does mean God takes careful note of what you care about, and it *will* make a difference in the next life. What kind of difference? I don't know. But I do know that we can never, never go wrong when we live to please God.

Enoch's life draws such interest because we know that he walked alive into the other side. It was like a solo rapture, where he was caught away to be with God—transferred into Heaven immediately.

Enoch went from walking with God to waking with God.

That could very well happen to us. I believe we are living in the last days, and that Jesus Christ could come back at any time. As far as I can see in my study of biblical prophecy, I believe the next event on the prophetic calendar is the rapture of the church, when all true followers of Jesus are caught up to meet Him in the air, in a moment, in the twinkling of an eye.

If, however, the Lord doesn't come in our lifetime, we will die. The statistics on death are really impressive. One out of every one persons will die. The Bible says, "It is appointed for men to die once, but after this the judgment" (Heb. 9:27). There is no escaping death before Jesus comes.

Here is the good news. Enoch walked with God on earth, therefore he was received by the Lord in Heaven. When you walk with God and death comes, you have nothing to fear. It's just the next step on your journey with Him.

The Bible tells us "to be absent from the body and to be present with the Lord" (2 Cor. 5:8). The moment you take your last breath on earth, you take your first breath in Heaven.

That was Enoch's experience, and that is the hope of the world changer.

Do you have that hope?

3

The World Changer at the End of the World

> He was warned about something he couldn't see, and
> acted on what he was told. . . . His act of faith drew a
> sharp line between the evil of the unbelieving world
> and the rightness of the believing world.
>
> ~Hebrews 11:7 MSG

Have you ever been in a really dark place and noticed what happens when a light turns on? Maybe you're in a theater and the movie has reached a crucial scene. The action gets intense, and as everyone leans forward a little to see what will happen, someone pulls out their phone to check messages or log on to Instagram.

It's like a little explosion of light, illuminating half the theater, and every head turns that way. It's an unwelcome distraction to say the least, because a little light goes a long way.

I saw an MIT study that proved the human eye can see a single candle flame over a mile and a half away on a dark night.[1] That's impressive, I guess, but somehow I think that distance must be even greater.

Have you ever been on a plane, maybe flying home from somewhere at night, sitting in a window seat, and looking out over the dark landscape? When you fly over a town or maybe even a lonely farm out on the prairie, you can see tiny twinkling lights far below. There you are at thirty thousand feet over Kansas or South Dakota, and your eyes spot a dusty sixty-watt bulb hanging from a post by a farmer's barn.

The darker it is outside, the more that light appears.

Imagine how dark it must have been hundreds or even thousands of years ago, before the invention of electricity or gas lanterns. In this chapter, we will read about a world changer who lived in a very, very dark period of history. It wasn't just dark after sunset, it was spiritually dark all day and all night. In fact, it was the darkest the world has ever been—yet still not as dark as it will be before the end. In the midst of this black and gloomy backdrop, a bright light shone, and that light could probably be seen for miles and miles—perhaps by everyone on the planet. The light came from the life of a true world changer. His name was Noah.

In the last chapter we considered Enoch, who lived in an even earlier era when evil was on the rise but hadn't yet overtaken the world. By Noah's day, that takeover was complete. If Enoch lived out his years in twilight, Noah lived at full midnight. In fact, Noah was a world changer who lived at the end of the world.

When I say the end of the world, I mean the end of that first, ancient world, in the time before the great flood wiped out all life on earth, sparing only Noah and his family.

Noah was a misunderstood character, and his story has been the subject of several movies over the years. Back in 2007, Steve Carrell played Noah for laughs in *Evan Almighty*. More recently Hollywood attempted an epic biblical-disaster blockbuster called *Noah* that starred Russell Crowe.

Noah was a curious movie, to say the least. There were moments that I thought were quite amazing, including the ark, the flood, and all the special effects. They were incredible to watch on the big screen. While the floodwaters were rising, the movie portrayed Noah trying to close the door of the ark with crowds of people trying to push their way in. And this Hollywood Noah is *killing* them. It's like Russell Crowe is the gladiator again, reverting back to Maximus Decimus Meridius and cutting down his enemies.

It's a very dramatic scene, but it never appears in the Bible. All the Bible says about Noah and the door of the ark is this: "The LORD shut him in" (Gen. 7:16). And that was that.

The Whole World Was against Him

When you think about it, Noah was the ultimate rebel. Why? Because outside of his wife and kids, he went against the grain of the *whole world*. Have you ever heard someone say, "The whole world is against me?" In Noah's case, that was literally true. He was devoted to God, followed after Him, stood his ground in the face of great ridicule and scorn, and did what God asked him to do—even when it didn't make much earthly sense.

The Hebrews 11 Hall of Faith says: "By faith Noah, being divinely warned of things not yet seen, moved with godly fear, prepared an ark for the saving of his household, by which he condemned the world and became heir of the righteousness which is according to faith" (v. 7).

Let's try to identify some principles that mark Noah as a world changer.

God Revealed Secrets to Noah

The verse we just read says that Noah was "divinely warned of things not yet seen." In other words, the Lord spoke to His servant and told him what was coming. As far as we know, Noah was the only man in the world who knew what the future held. Noah heard the Word of God and simply believed it.

Has God spoken to you lately? Has He revealed anything to you? Someone might ask, "How does God speak?" First of all, He speaks primarily through His Word, the Bible. Romans 10:17 says, "Faith comes by hearing, and hearing by the word of God." When you open the Word of God—read it, study it, and think about it—you will hear His voice in your heart and in your thoughts.

At other times, the Lord might speak through your pastor or a friend. Sometimes He will speak through a wife or a husband! He may also speak through circumstances or in a quiet moment in the stillness of your heart. Although God can and does speak with an audible voice on occasion, He normally doesn't do that. Even so, He speaks often. He even speaks through His creation.

The heavens declare the glory of God;
    the skies proclaim the work of his hands.
Day after day they pour forth speech;
    night after night they reveal knowledge.
They have no speech, they use no words;
    no sound is heard from them.
Yet their voice goes out into all the earth,
    their words to the ends of the world. (Ps. 19:1–4
    NIV)

Perhaps you have experienced a time in your life when you felt like the Lord was nudging you in some direction—possibly to do or say something you weren't sure you wanted to do or say. There was no booming voice from Heaven or celestial music, but deep down, you were pretty sure it was the Lord prompting you to take a step you felt reluctant to take. Maybe it was apologizing to someone. Maybe it was making a call to someone you hadn't been speaking to. Maybe it was doing some good turn for someone you normally wouldn't have paid attention to.

That happens with me sometimes. I know the Lord is speaking to me, though I don't hear any words. It's an inner nudge in a certain direction. Sometimes it's a person I feel that He wants me to speak to. When I respond and walk over to that individual, I have no idea what I'm going to say. I just start talking and the Lord gives me direction and words.

God may be nudging you to try something outside your current comfort zone—like starting a Bible study with someone at work. The words He wants you to use are already forming in your mind, even though your feet feel cemented to the floor. Or maybe He is leading you to speak up and

share your faith in Christ with someone. You may not have heard an audible voice speaking over your right shoulder. The ground didn't tremble, bushes didn't burn, and no angels appeared. But you couldn't escape the conviction that it was really God speaking to you.

Did you listen? Did you take note of what He said?

God spoke to Noah, revealing secrets to him, and he listened. Here's something we need to consider. Christians know things the world doesn't know. The newest or youngest believer knows more than many of the greatest academics and intellectuals of the world, because he or she believes what God says in His Word.

The psalmist wrote: "Your commands make me wiser than my enemies. . . . Yes, I have more insight than my teachers, for I am always thinking of your laws. I am even wiser than my elders, for I have kept your commandments" (Ps. 119:98, 99–100 NLT).

Jesus confirms this in Matthew 11:25, "I thank You, Father, Lord of heaven and earth, that You have hidden these things from the wise and prudent and have revealed them to babes." Even the humblest believer knows more than many of the most educated people of the world with all their advanced degrees.

We know and firmly believe things that the world refuses to acknowledge. We know where human life began and where the universe came from. We know that humankind is not basically good but rather sinful, and that is why we need a Savior. We know that conditions in our world will become much, much worse before they become better. We know for sure that Jesus Christ is coming back again and that good will ultimately prevail. In spite of everything hell might throw

at us, we know that righteousness will win in the end. Not everyone knows that, but Christians do.

God revealed His secrets to Noah, and He will reveal His secrets to you too.

Noah Had Great Reverence for God

Hebrews 11:7 speaks of Noah being "moved with godly fear." Sometimes that word *fear* in Scripture seems a little puzzling to us. Are we talking about the kind of fear that makes us want to run and hide? The Bible says that "The fear of the LORD is the beginning of wisdom" (Prov. 9:10). When we talk about fearing God, does it mean we're afraid He's going to smack us if we take one step out of line?

No, what it really means is that we have *reverence* for Him.

One definition of fearing God says that rather than a fear of retribution, it is a wholesome dread of displeasing Him. I don't want to dishonor Him. I don't want to disappoint Him. I don't want to cause Him grief or lose the sense of His companionship.

Noah was moved with this reverence and fear, and I think we can learn from that. Sometimes I think the way people speak about the Lord is way too casual. While enjoying a relationship with God, they forget who He is—the God who is the very definition of holiness. This isn't your big buddy in the sky, this is the living God we're talking about. The Almighty. In the Lord's Prayer, Jesus taught us right off the bat to pray, "Our Father in heaven, Hallowed be Your name" (Luke 11:2). In other words, *reverenced* be Your name, *holy* is Your name.

We should never lose our reverence and awe of God. Yes, He allows us the incredible privilege of calling Him Father,

and Jesus has acknowledged us as His friends. But when we pray, we should never forget who it is we're speaking to.

Years ago I had the opportunity to become friends with the amazing British author, theologian, and preacher Dr. Alan Redpath. He was a wonderful gentleman who is now in Heaven. Cathe and I admired him so much that we named one of our sons after him: Jonathan Alan Laurie. We invited Dr. Redpath to our church to speak, and I had the privilege to spend quite a bit of time with him. I was always a little in awe of him. When we were together, I didn't goof around as much as I do with others, and I always called him Dr. Redpath.

He would shake his head and say in that distinctive British accent, "Oh Greg, don't call me Dr. Redpath. Call me Alan." And I would reply, "Anything you say, Dr. Redpath." I had such respect for him that I never felt comfortable calling him by his first name, and I never did.

I think of the apostle Paul, who knew God very well and was privileged both to speak to Jesus on the road to Damascus and to be caught up to Heaven for a brief visit before being returned to earth (see 2 Cor. 12:1–4). Paul knew God well, yet every now and then in his letters he seemed to look up from what he was writing and express overwhelming wonder and awe about who God is. When writing to his young friend Timothy, he suddenly broke out with these words: "At just the right time Christ will be revealed from heaven by the blessed and only almighty God, the King of all kings and Lord of all lords. He alone can never die, and he lives in light so brilliant that no human can approach him. No human eye has ever seen him, nor ever will. All honor and power to him forever! Amen" (1 Tim. 6:15–16 NLT).

Noah Understood God's Righteousness

Like Paul, Noah had a close relationship with the Lord, just as Enoch did before him. But Noah understood very well (who better?) that the Lord was a holy and righteous God who would judge sin.

And as far as Noah and the Lord were concerned, sin was *everywhere*.

In Genesis 6:5–7, we read these amazing words:

> Then the Lord saw that the wickedness of man was great in the earth, and that every intent of the thoughts of his heart was only evil continually. And the Lord was sorry that He had made man on the earth, and He was grieved in His heart. So the Lord said, "I will destroy man whom I have created from the face of the earth, both man and beast, creeping thing and birds of the air, for I am sorry that I have made them."

The world didn't reflect occasional evil or even frequent evil. It was *only* evil. As God looked into the minds of everyone on the planet, there wasn't even a single passing thought that was worthy, kind, or good. It was just evil layered upon evil layered upon evil.

Years ago Cathe and I were in New York City during a garbage strike. Bad timing on our part! All the trash collectors in the Big Apple stayed home for weeks, and garbage began to pile up everywhere. On some streets you could hardly find the sidewalks. It was trash piled on top of trash. The only New York residents who seemed to be enjoying the situation were the rats, and there were plenty of them. It was a disgusting mess, and the smell was so bad it would almost gag you.

That was Noah's world before the flood. Morally and spiritually, it stunk to high Heaven. And God, after surveying what His world had become, actually said, "I'm sorry that I even made mankind."

There is one part of Genesis 6:6 that you don't want to miss. We read that God was *grieved* He had made humankind. Another translation says that "it broke his heart" (NLT).

Consider this. You only grieve for those you love. If a stranger insults you, you just shake it off. It might make you a little angry, but you don't grieve over their words. On the other hand, when someone you love insults you, when a family member disappoints you, or when someone you care about does something hurtful and bad, you do grieve. You grieve over people you care about. Your heart breaks because of people you love.

Sometimes people read about God bringing judgment on the world, and they say, "That doesn't make sense. Why would a loving God bring judgment on us?"

Here is the answer. God is certainly loving. The Bible tells us that His very name is love. But He is also just. As Abraham said in Genesis 18:25, "Shall not the Judge of all the earth do right?" And speaking of doing right, if humans continue to flagrantly and continually break God's laws by murdering, destroying, and perverting everything that is wholesome and good, should God just turn His back and do nothing? Actually, *that* would make no sense. God is loving and good and kind and faithful. And He is also holy and just.

Let's imagine your little toddler is playing in the backyard when a wolf suddenly bounds over the fence and comes toward your child with fangs bared. What would you do? Would you kill the wolf? Of course you would. For the love of your child you would destroy the thing that was about to destroy him. In many ways this is similar to how God will deal with evil on the day He brings judgment.

Does God enjoy judging and punishing? Actually, He doesn't. In Ezekiel 33:11, He says: "As surely as I live . . . I take no pleasure in the death of wicked people. I only want them to turn from their wicked ways so they can live. Turn! Turn from your wickedness, O people of Israel! Why should you die?" (NLT).

God is saying, in effect, "I don't want these consequences to fall on you. I don't want you to suffer these things. But if you don't repent, if you don't change your mind about the direction in which you're heading, it's going to happen to you. And you will be bringing it on yourself."

Even though Noah certainly lived in a cultural cesspool, an anything goes sort of world, he never lost his grip on the character of God. He may have been the only one on the planet to know about the holy God, but he held onto that knowledge with all his heart and soul. The old world was about to sink beneath the waves, but Noah's example would set a fresh standard for the one that would emerge.

Noah Found Grace in the Eyes of the Lord

Genesis 6:8 says, "Noah found grace in the eyes of the LORD." Does that mean God poured grace upon Noah because He lived a righteous life? No. It means the very opposite. Noah lived a righteous life *because* God had grace on him. What is grace? It has been defined as God's unmerited favor. Because he found grace, or grace found him, Noah lived a righteous life.

God does not love us for what we have or haven't done. God loves us and extends grace and favor toward us because He chooses to, in His great love.

Noah responded appropriately to that grace, obeying and honoring the Lord, and became a world changer.

Noah Walked with God When No One Else Did

Genesis 6:9 says, "Noah walked with God." Like his great-grandfather, Enoch, Noah responded to God's grace and walked with Him. By the way, it is only said that four people in all the Bible walked with God. It's not that others didn't because, as I noted, Adam had his daily encounters with God in the garden of Eden, but only four people have those words printed below their portraits in the Bible.

Enoch, Noah, Abraham, and Zacharias.

Do you suppose Noah thought about the example of his ancestor Enoch and tried to emulate it? It seems like a good bet, doesn't it? I want that in my life too. By God's grace, I want my son Jonathan and my grandchildren to know that I tried to honor and follow God in my life. I want to live a legacy of faith for them to follow.

In the previous chapter we talked about Amos 3:3: "Can two walk together, unless they are agreed?" Again, the idea conveyed there is keeping in step with God. It means conforming your will to His will and seeking to honor Him. Noah had that sort of walk with God but, outside of his little family, no one else in the world did.

Do you ever feel a little lonely in your walk with the Lord? Maybe you feel like you're the only one at your work or in your school or in your neighborhood who wants to love and serve the Lord. That's one of the reasons I love our Harvest Crusades, which are large-scale evangelistic events in large arenas and stadiums. One of their greatest features, in addition to thousands of people coming to Christ, is that thousands of Christians gather together in one place to worship God together. It's hard to describe what it's like unless you have experienced it. It reminds you that you're not alone. There are hundreds and thousands of believers with you on this walk of faith. Yes, we sometimes feel like we are a minority. And in many ways, we are. But it's good to remember that there are believers—sometimes quiet, sometimes hidden—all around us.

The great prophet Elijah felt like he was the only one serving the Lord in his era. Once, when he was in a place of real fear and distress, he cried out to the Lord: "I have been very zealous for the LORD God of hosts; because the children of Israel have forsaken Your covenant, torn down Your altars, and killed Your prophets with the sword. I alone am left; and they seek to take my life" (1 Kings 19:14).

We all have those Elijah moments in our lives—times when we can't see beyond our own anxiety, loneliness, or depression—when our world and our options seem very, very limited. But the Lord has no such restrictions. He can see what we can't, and He has resources beyond our imaginations that He's ready to use on our behalf. In response to Elijah's meltdown, the Lord told him, "I'm preserving for myself seven thousand souls: the knees that haven't bowed to the god Baal, the mouths that haven't kissed his image" (1 Kings 19:18 MSG).

The Lord was saying, "Snap out of it, Elijah. There are plenty of people who still love and serve Me. You're not the only one." And then the Lord, in His kindness, brought Elijah a friend and companion named Elisha to carry his burden with him.

Noah didn't have any buddies he could grab coffee with in that godless world before the flood. He didn't have a good neighbor raking leaves in the next yard—someone he could chat with and say, "Can you believe what's going on these days?" But he had one best friend who walked with him every day and never left his side. So do we, and He's just a prayer away.

Noah Was a Witness for God

Did you know that the apostle Peter wrote about Noah? In 2 Peter 2:5, we read that God "did not spare the ancient world when he brought the flood on its ungodly people, but protected Noah, a preacher of righteousness" (NIV).

So besides being a shipbuilder, Noah was a preacher. But the evangelistic side of his ministry wasn't going very well. The Bible tells us that he went one hundred and twenty years without winning a single convert. Noah faithfully let his light shine in that dark, bitter world, but no one responded. No one listened, no one paid him any heed, and no one changed. If he lived today, he would have no followers on Twitter, zero friends on Facebook, and not one soul would "like" his posts.

Discouraging as that may have been, Noah probably understood that converting people wasn't his job. His job was to be a preacher of righteousness, declaring God's message, whether people responded or not. It's the same for you and me and every other believer. Our job isn't to convert people.

In fact, I have never and will never convert anyone. Nor will you! That is the work of God's Spirit.

Sometimes my job as a pastor and evangelist is just to sow the seed—to put the message out there to the best of my ability. Occasionally I have the privilege of reaping a harvest where others have watered and sown and tended the seed for a long time. The bottom line is that I am called to be a faithful witness.

And that is your bottom line as well. Be faithful with what the Lord has set before you. Take advantage of the opportunities and openings God has brought your way. God won't hold you accountable for what He has called me to do, and He won't hold me accountable for the tasks He has placed at your feet. Do what you can while you can.

I love the J. B. Phillips translation of Ephesians 5:15–16: "Live life, then, with a due sense of responsibility, not as men who do not know the meaning and purpose of life but as those who do. Make the best use of your time, despite all the difficulties of these days. Don't be vague, but firmly grasp what you know to be the will of God."

Even though Noah never reached any outsiders with his example or his preaching, he did reach his own family. "By faith Noah, being divinely warned of things not yet seen, moved with godly fear, prepared an ark for the saving of his household" (Heb. 11:7).

Maybe he didn't reach thousands . . . or hundreds . . . or even a handful. But he reached his family. They believed and helped him build that crazy ark out in the middle of a field somewhere, perhaps miles from any body of water. They might have had their doubts—just as we all do—but they knew that their dad loved God and walked with Him. They knew that he was a man of integrity.

This is a message to parents in an era that's rapidly growing as dark as the ancient world. God has given you the responsibility to raise your children in the way of the Lord, and you must not fail in this mission. It's simply not acceptable to say you're too busy to read the Bible to your kids before they go to sleep at night. It's no good to say you don't have time to take your kids to church and make sure they're in a good children's or youth program. Again, if you want to change the world, you have to start with your world. And to do that, you should begin with those closest to you—your children.

Time passes incredibly fast. Soon they will be older, and your influence will not be as strong as when they were young.

Hopefully, your church will reinforce what you are already teaching and modeling at home. When should you teach your children? *Constantly.* Make use of every opportunity. Moses wrote: "You must think constantly about these commandments I am giving you today. You must teach them to your children and talk about them when you are at home or out for a walk; at bedtime and the first thing in the morning" (Deut. 6:6–7 TLB).

It is such a joy when your kids finally "get it," isn't it? Yes, they will go through their phases, and they may even rebel for a time. Then hopefully one day—maybe even a long way down the road—the truth sinks in and they start turning toward the Lord.

My youngest son, Jonathan, was a prodigal just as his older brother, Christopher, was before he got serious about pursuing God. Jonathan recommitted his life to the Lord after God suddenly called his brother home to Heaven in an automobile accident. It was a statement that Christopher made to Jonathan that really shook his life. One of the last things Christopher said to his younger brother was, "What is it going to take for you to commit your life to Jesus Christ?" After Christopher went to Heaven, Jonathan got serious about his faith. He's now a pastor, teaching the Word of God and preaching the gospel.

What's even better than that is seeing Jonathan's faith continuing into the next generation. Not long ago he was getting his little daughter Allie ready for her first day of public school. He said to her, "Allie, not everybody in the school where you are going believes in Jesus. Do you understand that? They don't all know Jesus or love Jesus like you do. We just need to pray that God will help you find friends."

Allie listened carefully and nodded her head to show that she understood. Then Jonathan prayed with her. When he was done, Allie added this little P.S. to the prayer. She said, "Lord, help me find some new friends. And if they don't know about Jesus, help me to tell them about Jesus."

There will be stormy times ahead in our nation and our world before Jesus comes back as the returning King. We need to do all that we can to bring the Gospel to our culture, because Jesus has commanded us to do so. But we must also make sure that our families find their way into the ark.

The Ark Had a Door

The Lord eventually closed the door on the ark Himself, as we saw in Genesis 7:16. But for a long time, during the ark's construction and while the animals were gathering to enter in, the door was open. Anyone could have gone in and found safety. Noah wasn't blocking the way and killing people gladiator-style like in the Hollywood version.

The sad truth was this. No one wanted to come in. No one believed God or His messenger. Finally, in Genesis 7:1, God said to Noah: "Come into the ark, you and all your household, because I have seen that you are righteous before Me in this generation."

That sounds to me like an invitation. He didn't say, "Go into the ark," He said, "Come." That's what I say when a guest comes to our front door. "Come on inside."

To me, *come* is one of the most beautiful words in the New Testament. When the Lord's first two disciples approached Him and said, "Rabbi, where are you staying?" Jesus replied, "Come, and you will see" (John 1:38, 39 NIV).

To Simon and Andrew in their fishing boat, He said, "Follow Me and I will make you fishers of men" (Matt. 4:19).

To everyone who has ever felt worried or weighed down by cares and troubles, He says, "Come to me, all you who are weary and burdened, and I will give you rest. Take my yoke upon you and learn from me, for I am gentle and humble in heart, and you will find rest for your souls" (Matt. 11:28–29 NIV).

And in the last chapter of the last book of the Bible, we hear this invitation, straight out of Heaven: "And the Spirit and the bride say, 'Come!' And let him who hears say, 'Come!' And let him who thirsts come. Whoever desires, let him take the water of life freely" (Rev. 22:17).

Many people don't take time to respond to the Lord's invitation until they're in the middle of a huge crisis. In the aftermath of the 9/11 attacks, churches were overflowing for a few weeks. People were frightened and horrified and wanted a spiritual perspective on what just happened. There were even prayer vigils on street corners in America's cities. Members of Congress spontaneously broke into "God Bless America" on the steps of the Capitol. But it ended almost as quickly as it started. As a nation, we pretty much went back to our normal busyness.

During the coronavirus pandemic, we have had to literally close the doors of our church building, but thousands of people have joined us electronically for our live services. On one occasion, over a million people watched! But as with the aftermath of the 9/11 attacks, I wonder if people will return to their old ways of lethargy once the crisis is over.

That happens in our lives too. There might be a crisis that causes us to call out to God. And because He is so gracious, He hears us and responds to us. He says, "Call to Me, and I will answer you, and show you great and mighty things, which you do not know" (Jer. 33:3).

He is waiting for us to call upon Him.

And for those who have never received Him or responded to His invitation, the door of the ark is still open.

He is the door. He said so. "I am the door. If anyone enters by Me, he will be saved" (John 10:9).

Noah and his little family walked through an open door, escaping the worst disaster the world had ever known, and found refuge, peace, and a precious opportunity to start life over again. We can do that too. When we take simple steps of obedience like Noah, who can even imagine how our loving, all-powerful God might change our world?

The World Changer with No Forwarding Address

By an act of faith, Abraham said yes to God's call to travel to an unknown place that would become his home. When he left he had no idea where he was going.

~Hebrews 11:8 MSG

These days most people have access to that incredible innovation of our time: GPS, the global positioning system. It's now in so many new cars, smartphones, and other devices that people have begun to take it for granted.

Actually, younger people today can hardly imagine a world without it. If you try to explain that people used to get their directions from a multifolded sheet of paper called a map, you get some blank stares. "How would you use such a thing?" they might say. "It doesn't even talk to you."

I've been bailed out by GPS too many times to count, but let's be honest. It has also misled me. Not long ago I was heading to an unfamiliar destination when the GPS's robotic voice told me to turn right off the freeway at the next off-ramp. I promptly obeyed. Then the voice had me turn right again, turn left, and turn right two more times. That put me back on the same freeway a few miles down the road, and the voice was satisfied. *What was that all about?* I never found out whether my GPS was directing me around some obstacle or just taking me through a random exercise for the fun of it.

Recently I read an article that detailed a few serious GPS misadventures. A woman in Boston was driving through town with her kids when her GPS told her to make an immediate right turn directly onto some railroad tracks. Then her car stalled. She quickly got herself and her kids out of the vehicle to safety, but a train hit her car.[1]

Another article tells a story just as scary.

A glitch in the Apple Maps app on newer iPhones and iPads guides people up to a runway at a major Alaska airport instead of sending them on the proper route to the terminal, an airport official said Wednesday.

The map actually stops at the tarmac, but twice this month, wayward drivers have continued across an active runway.

"It doesn't actually tell you to cross, but the problem is, people see the terminal then at that point, because they are right there . . . they just continue across," said Fairbanks International Airport spokeswoman Angie Spear.[2]

The lesson here, I guess, is that you can't outrun a 747. Do not pull your car onto a runway!

I also read about an elderly couple who became stranded after their GPS directed them onto a back road where their car got stuck. They spent two nights in the wilderness before, thankfully, they were rescued.

Again, what does GPS stand for? Maybe *Get Potentially Stranded*. I know that I need it, because I have no navigational skills whatsoever and would constantly get lost without it. But as with so many other wonderful innovations of modern life, we have to remember that it isn't perfect, and that it can lead us into trouble if we're not on our toes or if we rely on it too heavily.

God was way ahead of the GPS innovation. Right from the beginning He created certain of His creatures with an amazing homing instinct, or what we might call a built-in GPS. One of the most mind-blowing examples to me is the golden plover, a native bird of Hawaii. During the summer the adult plovers migrate to the Aleutian Islands, some 1,200 miles away from their sunnier habitat. In the Aleutians, the birds mate, the females lay their eggs, and the little ones are hatched. Then unaccountably, Mom and Dad say, "See ya, kids. We're out of here. Be good. Bye." And they leave the little fledglings hanging out in the Aleutians.[3]

Something about that doesn't seem right. The adult plovers don't even leave their fledglings with little smartphones. They don't even send them a Tweet. (I think birds should be able to send a Tweet. Don't you?)

But somehow, in God's plan, it all works out. The little birds *know* that the Aleutians are not where they ultimately belong. They *know* they are supposed to launch out for somewhere they have never been before. So they take off for Hawaii—and they get there too. How do they do it? How do they find it? They can do these things because God has placed a homing instinct within them. The way to Hawaii is imprinted in their little brains. By the way, the next time someone calls you a birdbrain you might take it as a compliment.

Of course, many of God's other creatures have the same ability, whether it's a dog, a cat, a humpback whale, or a monarch butterfly. Not long ago I read the story of Pero, a four-year-old working sheepdog who somehow found his way from Cumbria, in northwest England, back to his previous home near Aberystwyth, on the coast of Wales—a distance of over 240 miles.[4]

We hear many such amazing stories of animals traveling great distances to arrive in a specific place. But what about human beings? Do we have a homing instinct as well?

I believe that we do, because human beings have been uniquely created in the image of God. From the moment we are born we are on a quest, looking for something that will satisfy a deep desire within.

We try all kinds of things to satisfy that deep-down gravitational pull. We can distract ourselves with all kinds of material stuff or anesthetize ourselves with drugs or alcohol or wear ourselves out doing all manner of things, but we can never be completely rid of that imprint on our souls. In the book of Ecclesiastes 3:11, the Bible says, "He has also set eternity in the human heart" (NIV). In other words, humans are hardwired to look for God and long for Heaven. We have an inborn instinct and a homesickness for a place we have never been before—just like those little plovers are drawn across a huge ocean toward islands they have never visited or seen.

Until we realize this truth, nothing on earth will really satisfy us. In his book *Mere Christianity*, author and theologian C. S. Lewis wrote, "If I find in myself a desire which no experience in this world can satisfy, the most probable explanation is that I was made for another world."[5]

In this chapter, we will look at a world changer named Abraham. Right in the middle of a settled and busy life, God called him to leave everything familiar and start out for a country and homeland he had never seen. And he did it. Abraham may have had a slow start, but he followed God's GPS signal into a new land and a life beyond what he had ever imagined.

"And He Went Out . . ."

Abraham has the biggest reputation of all those mentioned in the Hebrews 11 Hall of Faith. And for good reason! God used him to illustrate the life of faith more than any other man or woman in Scripture. Here is what the Lord highlights for us in Hebrews 11.

> By faith Abraham obeyed when he was called to go out to the place which he would receive as an inheritance. And he went out, not knowing where he was going. By faith he dwelt in the land of promise as in a foreign country, dwelling in tents with Isaac and Jacob, the heirs with him of the same promise; for he waited for the city which has foundations, whose builder and maker is God.
>
> By faith Sarah herself also received strength to conceive seed, and she bore a child when she was past the age, because she judged Him faithful who had promised. Therefore from

one man, and him as good as dead, were born as many as the stars of the sky in multitude—innumerable as the sand which is by the seashore. (vv. 8–12)

Did you know that Abraham is named seventy-four times in the New Testament? There are only eleven chapters of Genesis devoted to the first two thousand years of human history, consisting of nineteen earlier generations. But there are fourteen chapters dedicated to the life of one man, Abraham. And here in Hebrews 11, one-third of the verses are devoted to Abraham and his wife, Sarah. That's a lot of ink. God must have wanted us to know about this man and to consider the example of his life. He was a great patriarch of the faith, but he wasn't perfect. In fact, he was every bit as human as you and me.

What was it, then, that made Abraham a world changer? What did he do?

Abraham Listened to God

World changers listen to God—as we have already seen in the lives of Enoch and Noah. The Message translation of Hebrews 11:8 puts it like this: "By an act of faith, Abraham said yes to God's call to travel to an unknown place that would become his home. When he left he had no idea where he was going."

He listened to God. But don't imagine that he was already a worshiper of the one true God or that he already had one foot in the kingdom of Heaven. He didn't. In fact, Abraham and Sarah—Abram and Sarai at that time—had very deep roots in a pagan culture. It was all they knew. Living in Ur of the Chaldees, everyone in Abraham's family worshiped false gods. Abraham was probably an idol worshiper himself. Despite this, God handpicked Abraham and came to him with what must have seemed like an outrageous request.

In Genesis 12:1–2 , God said to Abraham, "Leave your own country behind you, and your own people, and go to the land I will guide you to. If you do, I will cause you to become the father of a great nation; I will bless you and make your name famous, and you will be a blessing to many others" (TLB).

The land I will guide you to.

God didn't tell him what or where that land was, or how long it would take to get there. He didn't tell him where or how they would live in that place. He basically said, "Leave everything you have ever known, follow Me, and don't leave a forwarding address." Ultimately, Abraham wasn't choosing to move to another country, he was choosing to follow the God who had spoken to him.

God leads us one step at a time, and that can be a little frustrating for us. Most of us would like to have a detailed blueprint early in life. *Lord, I need to know who I will marry. I need to know where I will live, what my profession will be, and how many children I will have. Will I live a long life, or die young?*

The Lord probably won't answer those questions in advance. He doesn't reveal things to us in one huge download. For one thing, He knows we would never be able to handle it. Beyond that, He wants us to learn to walk with Him and trust Him, one step at a time.

The Next Step of Obedience

I'm reminded of one of my favorite New Testaments stories. It can be found in the book of Acts, and it's about the only man who was identified as an evangelist. His name was Philip. As the story begins, Philip was leading a red-hot evangelistic crusade in Samaria. Philip was preaching, people were being healed, and demons were on the run, coming out of people with shrieks and fleeing to wherever demons flee. Acts 8:8 says that "there was great joy in that city."

Then right in the middle of this great revival and joy, an angel of the Lord appeared to Philip with some puzzling instructions. The angel told him, "Arise and go toward the south along the road which goes down from Jerusalem to Gaza" (Acts 8:26).

In other words, "Go to the desert. Now."

That's it? That's all he said? The angel didn't say, "Go to the desert and there will be a guy from Ethiopia searching for God and reading from Isaiah 53, so brush up on that." No. The angel simply said, "There's the road. Get going."

Philip could have argued and said, "Why should I go to the desert? You have opened all kinds of doors right here. We're having great meetings. This makes no sense." But if he said those things, the Bible doesn't record them. What we read is, "So he arose and went."

Like Abraham, Philip went in obedience and faith, not knowing his purpose or destination. But there he was in the desert, under a blazing sun, probably wishing he'd brought an extra bottle of water and some sunscreen. He might have said, "Why in the world am I here? Am I supposed to preach to lizards?"

Then he noticed a cloud of dust in the distance. As it got closer, he saw that it was a large entourage of people coming down the desert road. As they drew nearer, he realized that a foreign dignitary was riding in the lead chariot.

Do you suppose it had little flags on it with Secret Service guys running alongside? Probably not, but Philip was beginning to get an inkling of why the Lord had sent him there.

This was a high-ranking dignitary from Ethiopia who had traveled many miles from his home to Jerusalem, searching for God, and now he was on his way home. As Philip approached the dignitary, he heard him reading some words from a scroll. Philip must have smiled as he recognized the familiar words of Isaiah 53.

I like how Philip stepped right up and greeted the man. He was saying, in effect, "Hey, how's it going? I just happened to be here in the desert—and I think I know why."

Scripture says that Philip asked him, "Do you understand what you are reading?"

"No, I actually don't," the official replied. "Can you help me?"

"Why, yes. As a matter of fact, I can." And he climbed up into the chariot and shared the gospel with the dignitary, showing him how Isaiah 53 was actually pointing to Jesus Christ, who would lay His life down on the cross for the sins of the world. Then Philip led that man to faith in Jesus Christ. The Ethiopian dignitary went on his way rejoicing, and God sent Philip to his next assignment.[6]

Here is my point. God didn't tell Philip what was coming. He didn't tell him what to expect or how to prepare. He just said, "Take the next step," and Philip obeyed in faith.

God did the same for Abraham. Is He doing the same with you? Is He leading you to attempt something unexpected or unfamiliar to you? For instance, has He nudged you to have a conversation with a certain person?

If so, you might reply, "I don't know what I would say." Don't worry about that. Take the next step of obedience. If you're following God's GPS signal, you don't need a road map.

World Changers Listen to God

Have you ever watched the *Dora the Explorer* cartoons? I have four granddaughters who used to love Dora, so I got into it too. I've already memorized the names of the characters and the theme song (which I can't get out of my head).

Here is the basic plot of every episode. Dora goes out on an adventure with her little monkey friend, Boots (who always wears red boots). They get lost. They are tracked by a fox named Swiper, who is always trying to mess up their plans. But not to worry. Dora has her monkey with her, and she has a singing map to lead her along. The map has its own little theme song about knowing the right way to get them where they need to go. The singing map leads her and Boots home and out of the clutches of Swiper. That is basically every single Dora adventure in a nutshell—or at least the episodes I've watched.

Abraham didn't have a singing map—or any map at all. But what he had was a directive from Heaven. God said go, and he went.

Remember, this was before anyone had the written Word of God. There were no Bibles in the bookstores or public library. There was no Old Testament and certainly no New Testament. We can assume that God spoke audibly to Abraham, telling him what to do and where to go.

Have you ever wished God would speak audibly to you? Wouldn't it be great if you could get up each morning, pour yourself a cup of coffee, sit in a sunny corner of your dining room, and listen to God speak instructions and counsel for the day? I'd even be happy to get a text from God on my iPhone. "Okay, Greg, here is the plan for today. At 8:30 I want you to be here, and at 10:22 I want you to be there."

"Right, Lord. I've got it. Check in with You later."

That's not how God communicates with us, of course, but the fact is He speaks to us all the time. The question is, are you listening? If you want to hear God speak, pick up your Bible and read it with an open heart. You probably won't hear God's voice if you don't open the Bible and, like young Samuel, say, "Speak, LORD, for your servant is listening" (1 Sam 3:9 NIV).

Many of us don't have a problem with the fact that God speaks. It's just that we don't always like what He has to say. I remember hearing Pastor Chuck Smith, who is now with the Lord, tell the story of his grandson, who said to his mother one night, "Mom, God never speaks to me."

His mom replied, "That's not true, son. God speaks to you all the time."

"Mom, I never hear Him."

Then his mom said, "Think about when you do something wrong, son, and you feel guilty about it. That can be God speaking to you."

There was a pause, and then the boy said, "Mom, God speaks to me all the time."

It's up to us to determine whether we will pay attention to what the Lord says. Jesus said, "My sheep hear My voice, and I know them, and they follow Me" (John 10:27). That's just what Enoch and Moses did and Abraham before them.

World changers are always listening to hear the voice of God.

World Changers Obey God

It's not enough to hear from God; we have to then respond to what He tells us. World changers obey God.

To his credit, Abraham obeyed God right on the spot. Whatever it meant to pull up roots in Ur—liquidating his assets, loading up an Ur-Haul, or whatever he had to do—Abraham got right on it without argument. This was faith in action.

It must have been scary for Abraham and Sarah to follow the voice of a God they had never known and head off with everything they had over the horizon. But as we know, it turned out very, very well for them—better than they could have dreamed. It's the same with us. As we obey the Lord, doing what He tells us to do and staying away from things He tells us to avoid, we realize that He has our best interests at heart and that He will protect us. In fact, the Bible says, "No good thing will He withhold from those who walk uprightly" (Ps. 84:11).

God told Abraham to make a clean break with his past—including his family. Again, His specific command was: "Get out of your country, from your family and from your father's house, to a land that I will show you" (Gen. 12:1). God commanded him to leave his people—everyone he knew. Why? The Bible doesn't specifically say. But I think it's a good bet that his family and friends in good ol' Ur were dragging Abraham and Sarah down. Their environment was not conducive to the kind of spiritual growth God had in mind for them. So He told them, "It's time to walk away."

And to their credit, they did because world changers obey God.

What kind of influence does your family have on you? Or maybe we could turn that question around. What kind of influence do you have on *them*? Again, are you a passive thermometer, just reflecting the moods and attitudes of those around you? Or are you a thermostat, changing your environment for the better?

A world changer sets the temperature and influences their surroundings. A person being changed by the world is concerned with the opinions of other people, bending this way and that like tall grass in the wind. What kind of influence do you have on others in your immediate circle?

Abraham's family was evidently dragging him down, and God said, in effect, "If you want to walk with Me, then you can't keep walking with them. You have to cut them loose and separate yourself."

It reminds me of the formula for happiness captured in the very first psalm. If you want to be a happy and blessed person, there are certain things that you should do—and other things you should *not* do. Psalm 1:1 says, "Blessed [or happy] is the man [or woman] who walks not in the counsel of the ungodly, nor stands in the path of sinners, nor sits in the seat of the scornful."

Do you want to be a happy, peaceful, upbeat person? Then don't hang around with ungodly people who pull you down with their sour attitudes and negativity.

I'm not saying that you necessarily should change your entire environment, and God may not be telling you to pull up stakes and leave Ur. You may have a family that has ungodly people in it. You may be in a workplace or a classroom or dorm around people who don't honor God or even believe in Him, and you may not be able to change those circumstances.

But there is a difference between people I am around by necessity and those with whom I choose to associate on my own time. *As much as possible, spend time with godly people.* Find friends who love the Lord and read their Bible, who will build you up in your faith and increase your appetite for spiritual things. Do your best to limit time with people who drag you down and decrease your appetite for spiritual things.

Happy people are also known for what they do. Psalm 1 continues: "But his delight is in the law of the LORD, and in His law he meditates day and night" (v. 2). I'm throwing this into the chapter on Abraham at no extra charge. If you want to be a happy, growing person, don't hang around godless, negative people, and spend as much time as you can reading, studying, and thinking about the Word of God.

World Changers Are Heavenly Minded Heavenly Citizens

Right in the midst of the Hebrews 11 description of Abraham, we encounter this heart-lifting, incredibly beautiful paragraph.

All these people died still believing what God had promised them. They did not receive what was promised, but they saw it all from a distance and welcomed it. They agreed that they were foreigners and nomads here on earth. Obviously people who say such things are looking forward to a country they can call their own. If they had longed for the country they came from, they could have gone back. But they were looking for a better place, a heavenly homeland. That is why God is not ashamed to be called their God, for he has prepared a city for them. (vv. 13–16 NLT)

Singer-songwriter Jim Reeves had it right when he sang, "This world is not my home, I'm just a passing through."[7] It's true. We are just passing through. The Bible says this about our lives on earth: "We are here for only a moment, visitors and strangers in the land as our ancestors were before us. Our days on earth are like a passing shadow, gone so soon without a trace" (1 Chron. 29:15 NLT).

We began this chapter talking about a homing instinct, an internal GPS that points us to a place we have never been and can only scarcely imagine. Christians have a longing for something the earth can never, never deliver. We know— instinctively—that our heart's desire and deepest longings will only be fulfilled in our Lord's presence in Heaven. Yes, we can experience earth at its best and savor some beautiful, joyful, golden moments with friends and loved ones. But even these "best of times" are only shadows—pale imitations—of greater things to come. We were created for something more. Much, much more. It was Augustine who said, "Thou has made us for Thyself, O Lord, and our heart is restless until it finds its rest in Thee."

Because of this homesickness for Heaven, we see the world for what it really is. And when I speak of the world, I don't mean planet earth, with all its natural beauties and marvels, flawed as it is by the fall of man and the curse that followed. There is still much to experience and enjoy in this life and in this world. But it will be unimaginably better when the new earth comes.

When I talk about the world, I'm speaking of a mentality and a culture that is heavily influenced by Satan, who seeks to manipulate us and lure us into living for ourselves and our destructive selfish desires. The apostle John puts it like this:

"For the world offers only a craving for physical pleasure, a craving for everything we see, and pride in our achievements and possessions. These are not from the Father, but are from this world. And this world is fading away, along with everything that people crave" (1 John 2:16–17 NLT).

As citizens of Heaven we are built for another place. We are like the people in Hebrews 11:16: "They desire a better, that is, a heavenly country. Therefore God is not ashamed to be called their God, for He has prepared a city for them."

Heaven is a real place for real people to do real things. Before He left the earth, Jesus said, "I go to prepare a place for you" (John 14:2). Heaven is a city. It's an actual location where people live, where commerce is done. Perhaps it's even a place where you can eat in a restaurant or go watch a concert or pursue the work you are there to do. It's not *like* a city, it *is* a city.

But Heaven is also a country. It's not *like* a country, it *is* a country. And it is a paradise. These are words the Bible uses, and it helps us to remember that we're headed to a real, solid place when we make our departure from this life. If you have misty, foggy, ghostly images of Heaven in your mind, get rid of them. Heaven is a prepared place for prepared people. Are you prepared?

I heard about a little boy who was out flying his kite. He had it attached to so many balls of string and it was up so high that he couldn't even see it. A man walked by and saw the boy holding the string. "What are you doing, boy?" he said.

"Flying my kite, mister."

The man said, "I can't even see your kite. How do you know it's still there?"

The boy answered, "I can feel its tug."

In the same way Christians feel the tug of Heaven—and especially so after someone we love has left the world and gone on ahead of us. That helps us to start thinking about eternal things more.

I want you to notice something else. Abraham lived in a tent, which meant he was always on the move. He never built a permanent home. That's interesting because the Bible says that we live in tents too—and I don't mean a literal Coleman four-person tent with a rain flap. The New Testament describes your body as a tent. In 2 Corinthians 5:1, Paul writes, "For we know that when this earthly tent we live in is taken down (that is, when we die and leave this earthly body), we will have a house in heaven, an eternal body made for us by God himself and not by human hands" (NLT). Peter, too, compared his body and earthly life to a tent: "I think it is right to refresh your memory as long as I live in the tent of this body, because I know that I will soon put it aside" (2 Pet. 1:13–14 NIV).

This body will eventually wear out. The tent will spring a few leaks, the poles will collapse, or the fabric will wear through and that will be that. This comes as a great revelation to some people—especially us baby boomers who were once the great youth generation. But that's okay. We know that time passes. We're getting closer to the Lord and closer to seeing Him with each passing day.

World Changers Live by Faith

The word *promise* is repeated twice in Hebrews 11:9. "By faith [Abraham] dwelt in the land of promise as in a foreign country, dwelling in tents with Isaac and Jacob, the heirs with him of the same promise."

World changers live on promises, not explanations.

They live by faith, not by sight.

They live on fact, not on feelings.

We recognize that our true citizenship is in Heaven. That isn't just positive-thinking happy talk, that is the Word of God, which stands forever and cannot be changed. Philippians 3:20 says, "But our citizenship is in heaven. And we eagerly await a Savior from there, the Lord Jesus Christ" (NIV).

When God called Abraham, He gave him a promise. And then it was up to Abraham to take hold of that promise, which he could not yet see. That is what faith does. Faith sees what could be, not just what is.

As I have stated earlier, faith is like a muscle. It needs to be used. If you neglect it, it will atrophy, but if you use it and apply it, it will grow stronger. That means there will be times when you step out of your comfort zone and take some risks. That is what world changers do. We read in Romans 4:20, "[Abraham] grew strong in faith" (NASB).

He *grew* strong in faith. That doesn't mean he was born that way. It doesn't even mean that he lived most of his life that way. In fact, the passage above provides a snapshot of Abraham when he was one hundred years old! After ten decades of life, he was growing strong in his faith and becoming a world changer. He was listening to God more, obeying God more, and living in a way that would count toward eternity.

God never allows us to use the excuses that we are too old or that we have already failed too much or blown our chances. If we are alive on earth today, we still have the opportunity to grow strong in faith.

Tell God you want that and let the transformation begin now.

The Choices of a World Changer

Seek the Kingdom of God above all else, and he will give you everything you need. "So don't be afraid, little flock. For it gives your Father great happiness to give you the Kingdom."

~Luke 12:31–32 NLT

Someone asked me recently, "Greg, what were some of the best decisions you ever made in your life?" Maybe they thought that would be a tough question for me. It wasn't. It was easy.

My number one best decision was accepting Jesus Christ into my life. There's no question about that. It was and is the best thing I ever did or will ever do.

Number two was marrying my wife, Cathe. No question at all. I would do it over again in a heartbeat.

Number three was not wearing the toupee that was custom made for me. This is a true story. My friend Dennis Agajanian had said to me, "Hey Buddy, I know a guy who makes these incredible toupees. He's a Christian. You've got to get one, they're really amazing."

"Uh . . . no thank you," I told him. "I can't wear a toupee."

It was like he never even heard me. "Buddy, I'll get one made for you. He'll do it for free."

Sure enough, this guy made me a toupee and sent it through FedEx. I knew it was custom made because on the underside it had a label that said, "Made for Pastor Greg Laurie," followed by, "Praise the Lord!" One evening Cathe and I were going to Costco and I said, "I'm going to wear this thing just for the fun of it!"

She rolled her eyes but didn't comment. When we got out of the car at Costco, however, the wind was blowing really hard, and the toupee kept lifting off the back of my head. I just envisioned that thing flying off and landing on someone's windshield in the parking lot. *Made for Pastor Greg Laurie.*

I put the toupee away and never got it out again. That was a very good decision.

Not long ago I was reading an article about some of the worst business decisions different companies have made through the years. Do you remember the 1982 movie *ET*? It was a huge hit for Paramount Studios, raking in over 790 million dollars of revenue. Before the movie was released, the director, Steven Spielberg, approached the Mars Candy Company, asking them if they would like to have their famous M&M candies featured in the movie. (The script called for a cute little alien who liked candy.)

The Mars executives turned him down. After hearing the plot of the proposed movie, they couldn't imagine the film doing very well at the box office. So Spielberg took his script over to the Hershey company and asked for permission to use Reese's Pieces, which they were happy to grant. As a result, the sales of Reese's Pieces went up 65 percent the same month the film was released.[1] It just may have put that candy on the map.

And in 1962 the executive at Decca Records was given the opportunity to audition a new band. He listened to them and wasn't that impressed, remarking that guitar groups were already on their way out. As a result, Capitol Records scooped up the band, and in the first year sold thirty-eight million dollars' worth of records. Since then, they have raked in a lot more.

You've probably heard of the band. They called themselves the Beatles.

Instead of getting in on the ground floor with the Fab Four, Decca selected another group: Brian Poole and the Tremeloes.[2] I'm sure they were a fine band, but to pass on The Beatles? It is considered one of the worst decisions in the history of the music industry. Guitar groups on their way out? In 1962? I would imagine that the executive who made that choice was soon on *his* way out.

Our history books are filled with bad, even tragic, decisions. If you know anything about California history, you might have heard about a group called the Donner Party. In April of 1846, even before the California Gold Rush, nearly ninety pioneers set out from Chicago to California. Many were on their way to my state back in those days. It wasn't an easy journey by any stretch of the imagination, but it was doable.

Brothers Jacob and George Donner were leading a wagon train. They began their journey on the California trail—the main route most people used to reach the Golden State. In November of that year, however, after many miles, trials, and tribulations, someone told the leaders about a shortcut through the Sierra Nevada Mountains that would supposedly get them to their destination sooner. Disaster followed when they were stranded by mountain snows. Forty out of the eighty-seven who set out froze to death or perished from starvation, and a number of the survivors actually turned to cannibalism.[3]

The decision to try an untried shortcut couldn't have turned out worse.

Every one of us will face the three C's of life: challenges, choices, and consequences. Those challenges may come in the form of opportunities or temptations. The hardest thing to learn in life is which bridges to cross and which bridges to burn, because our choices will shape our destiny.

In this chapter, we will consider two believers, Abraham and Lot, whose lives demonstrate that principle. For the most part, Abraham made right choices in life. His nephew Lot made a series of wrong and disastrous choices that he lived to deeply regret. As a result, one became a world changer, and the other was changed by the world.

God will be there for us and help us when we come to a fork in the road and face a major life decision. The Bible promises that God will give us wisdom when we ask for it (see James 1:5), but it's still up to each one of us to follow through on what He reveals.

Choose Life

My granddaughter Allie loves school. It's her third year in public school, and she can't get enough of it. Not long ago her sister, who attends another school, was off for the day. Cathe and I were babysitting them and we told Allie she could take the day off from school to be with her sister. When I was in school, I would have jumped at the chance for a day off. But not Allie. She said, "No. I want to go to school."

I looked at her and thought, *Are you even related to me? How did this happen?* God gives tests to each of His followers in life.

In Deuteronomy 30:19–20, the Lord essentially gives all of us an open-book test. Here is what He says.

> This day I call the heavens and the earth as witnesses against you that I have set before you life and death, blessings and curses. Now choose life, so that you and your children may live and that you may love the LORD your God, listen to his voice, and hold fast to him. For the LORD is your life. (NIV)

I love that. God says, "Here is your choice. I'm putting it before you. You can choose life or death. Blessings or curses. Oh, and by the way, the right response is to choose life. If you make that choice, you will be very, very glad you did. See, I'm giving you the answer right up front. But it's still your decision to make."

It is so true. God says choose life so that you *and your children* may live. Your choices will affect not only you but your children and potentially your grandchildren and great-grandchildren. Selfish, ungodly decisions can impact a family for generations. By the same token, godly decisions can bring great blessings to a family for generations as well.

Now let's look at two men whose lives illustrate both sides of that equation.

The First Right Choice

Let's review what the Hall of Faith has to say about Abraham:

> By faith Abraham obeyed when he was called to go out to the place which he would receive as an inheritance. And he went out, not knowing where he was going. By faith he dwelt in the land of promise as in a foreign country, dwelling in tents with Isaac and Jacob, the heirs with him of the same promise. (Heb. 11:8–9)

Scripture calls Abraham "the friend of God" several times.[4] When did that friendship begin? It may have started on the day when God spoke to Abraham and called him into a completely new life. Up to that point, God hadn't been on Abraham's radar—although Abraham had always been on God's. The Lord told His friend that He wanted him to leave his life of paganism and the worship of false gods. It was time, God said, for Abraham and Sarah to pack their bags and get out of Dodge, leaving all their extended family behind.

Abraham trusted this God who had spoken to him (that's what friends do), so he loaded the U-Haul and left Ur in the rearview mirror. That was a right choice, and it set the tone for the rest of his life.

The First Wrong Choice

But Abraham also made the decision to take one family member with him—a choice he would live to regret. Abraham's nephew Lot was trouble, and he brought stress and adversity into his uncle's life.

It's not that different for us. We know people who encourage us in our faith and build us up spiritually. But we also know people who have the opposite effect and tend to drag us down. If we go out for dinner with one couple, we come away feeling encouraged and refreshed. When we spend time with certain other people, however, we end up wishing we hadn't.

I think of all the people I have had the opportunity to meet and get to know through the years—so many wonderful, godly men and women who have marked my life and continue to do so. I suppose if I had to narrow it down to the godliest person I have ever met and spent time with, it would hands-down be Billy Graham. Now with the Lord, he was the most Christlike person I have ever met. Unbelievably kind. Unfailingly generous. He was everything you ever thought he was and more. I will never be Billy Graham, but I would love to have that kind of positive impact on the people in my world.

On the other side of the coin, I know Christians who seem to walk around perpetually angry. They frown a lot, they're openly cynical, and they always seem mad at someone about something. They remind me of Don Quixote tilting at windmills and getting nowhere. They always have to have some adversary or nemesis they're grumbling about. People like that—who are always upset, always sour, and always sarcastic—make me tired. After being with them for a while, I feel like I need to take a shower.

Some people pull you down and, after you've spent time with them, you do not look forward to being with them again. Other people build you up and help you feel closer to the Lord and encouraged in your walk of faith.

Lot was one of those guys that was dragging Abraham down. In 2 Timothy 2:22, Paul writes to his young friend: "Run from anything that stimulates youthful lusts. Instead, pursue righteous living, faithfulness, love, and peace. *Enjoy the companionship of those who call on the Lord with pure hearts*" (NLT, emphasis mine).

Having said that, this doesn't mean we should avoid all relationships with nonbelievers. Again, Paul writes in 1 Corinthians 5:9–11, "When I wrote to you before, I told you not to associate with people who indulge in sexual sin. But I wasn't talking about unbelievers who indulge in sexual sin, or are greedy, or cheat people, or worship idols. You would have to leave this world to avoid people like that. I meant that you are not to associate with anyone who claims to be a believer yet indulges in sexual sin, or is greedy, or worships idols, or is abusive, or is a drunkard, or cheats people. Don't even eat with such people" (NLT).

I *expect* nonbelievers to behave like nonbelievers. I'm not shocked when I'm working out at the gym and some guy turns the air blue with profanity. What am I supposed to do? Am I going to turn on him and say, "I can't believe you said that! Why aren't you more Christlike?"

Of course not. He can't be Christlike because he doesn't know Christ yet! And because I want him to know Jesus, I try to engage him and establish a dialogue with him, hoping to one day reach him for the Lord. I don't expect him to exhibit the behavior of a follower of Jesus.

When I'm around a Christian, however, I expect more. When I'm with someone who professes to be a follower of Christ, I am hoping they will reflect that in the way they speak and live and do business.

In the dynamic story before us, Abraham's nephew Lot was a believer in God—but a compromising one. Ultimately, Abraham had to put some distance between them.

Why did Abraham bring Lot along in the first place? It was probably because Lot's dad, Abraham's brother, had died, and Lot looked to his Uncle Abraham as a father figure. To Abraham's credit, there was something in this great patriarch that Lot really admired. He wanted to be around this godly man—and that's not all bad, is it?

A Parting of Ways

After an unwise and nearly disastrous detour into Egypt (see Gen. 12:10–20), Abraham got back on track and returned to the land God had called him to. And that is when the conflict with Lot began.

> So Abram left Egypt and traveled north into the Negev, along with his wife and Lot and all that they owned. (Abram was very rich in livestock, silver, and gold.) From the Negev, they continued traveling by stages toward Bethel, and they pitched their tents between Bethel and Ai, where they had camped before. This was the same place where Abram had built the altar, and there he worshiped the LORD again.
>
> Lot, who was traveling with Abram, had also become very wealthy with flocks of sheep and goats, herds of cattle, and many tents. But the land could not support both Abram and Lot with all their flocks and herds living so close together. So disputes broke out between the herdsmen of Abram and Lot. (At that time Canaanites and Perizzites were also living in the land.)

Finally Abram said to Lot, "Let's not allow this conflict to come between us or our herdsmen. After all, we are close relatives! The whole countryside is open to you. Take your choice of any section of the land you want, and we will separate. If you want the land to the left, then I'll take the land on the right. If you prefer the land on the right, then I'll go to the left."

Lot took a long look at the fertile plains of the Jordan Valley in the direction of Zoar. The whole area was well watered everywhere, like the garden of the LORD or the beautiful land of Egypt. (This was before the LORD destroyed Sodom and Gomorrah.) Lot chose for himself the whole Jordan Valley to the east of them. He went there with his flocks and servants and parted company with his uncle Abram. So Abram settled in the land of Canaan, and Lot moved his tents to a place near Sodom and settled among the cities of the plain. But the people of this area were extremely wicked and constantly sinned against the LORD. (Gen. 13:1–13 NLT)

Here is the operative statement we can draw from this portion of Scripture: *You make your choices and then your choices make you.*

Abraham and Lot had both become prosperous, acquiring great wealth. And there is nothing wrong with prospering! If you work hard, live a life of integrity, save your money, invest wisely, and make sure that you tithe and honor the Lord with your giving, it is very likely that you will do well financially. It doesn't necessarily mean you'll be rich, but the Lord will take care of you and meet your needs. God will bless you as you honor biblical principles. It shouldn't come as a shock that God would bless someone. Lot prospered and Abraham prospered.

The way that the older man and his young nephew reacted to this prosperity, however, was very different. Abraham had possessions, but possessions had Lot. It just comes down to how a person responds to God's gracious gifts. Some people may have a great abundance in their lives, but they are not that attached to it. They understand that wealth is a passing thing and that the Lord could take it back if He desired. Their touch on possessions is light. Others, however, hang on to everything with a white-knuckle grip. They pinch every penny and even hoard what they have.

I'm reminded of Gollum in *The Lord of the Rings*. Remember how he called his magical gold ring "my precious," and clung to it with an iron grip.

That was Lot. In reality, the problems and disputes between uncle and nephew weren't caused by the land or the wealth or even by the bickering herdsmen. The heart of every problem is the problem of the heart. Lot's heart was in this world, as evidenced by where he ended up living. Abraham was content with his lot, but Lot wanted a lot more! Lot wanted stuff. Abraham wanted God.

What do you want? What's the strongest, controlling desire of your heart? If you seek God first, if you seek Christ and His kingdom first, what does Jesus promise? "But seek first his kingdom and his righteousness, and all these things will be given to you as well" (Matt. 6:33 NIV).

If your life is all about acquiring stuff, getting ahead, being successful, or making a name for yourself, you will end up losing twice. You won't get the Lord, and you very likely won't get the stuff you were grasping for. And even if you do manage to get it, you probably won't be satisfied with it. You will just want more and more.

That was the problem with Lot. He wanted to have all this world offers, but he still wanted friendship with God. The Bible warns us in James 4:4, "You adulterers! Don't you realize that friendship with the world makes you an enemy of God? I say it again: If you want to be a friend of the world, you make yourself an enemy of God" (NLT).

So make a decision. Do you want to be God's friend or do you want to be the world's friend? Lot wanted to be the world's friend. Abraham wanted to be God's friend.

In reality, Lot wanted to have it both ways. The New Testament actually identifies Lot as a believer. But his conflicting priorities were tearing him apart. Read this incredible description in the book of 2 Peter.

> God condemned the cities of Sodom and Gomorrah and turned them into heaps of ashes. He made them an example of what will happen to ungodly people. But God also rescued Lot out of Sodom because he was a righteous man who was sick of the shameful immorality of the wicked people around him. Yes, Lot was a righteous man who was tormented in his soul by the wickedness he saw and heard day after day. (2:6–8 NLT)

Lot had foolishly moved close to Sodom—and then actually into Sodom—but he hated it! It was like a fly taking up residence near a spider's web. He hated the evil and immorality all around him. He had wealth and land and all he thought he had wanted, but it brought him no joy at all. In fact, he felt tormented every day.

While they were still together, Lot had leaned on Abraham, happy to live in the shelter and stability of his uncle's faith. Abraham walked with God, but Lot walked with Abraham. Lot needed Uncle Abe to hold him up and keep him going. He couldn't do it on his own. Why? Because he hadn't developed his own close relationship with the Lord!

I know people like this, and you probably do too. They might know the Lord and have a little knowledge from growing up in the church, but their hold on faith is weak. They rely on strong believers around them to keep them on track, drawing on *their* example and *their* faith. But they have never developed their own walk with Christ or learned how to endure trials or stand against Satan's attacks by using the Lord's strength. As a result, when they find themselves in deep trouble or facing a strong temptation, they fold up like a tent in the wind.

Lot was drawn to the bright lights and glamour of the world—not understanding how dark and vile and hateful the underbelly of that world could be. By the time he finally realized the truth, it was almost too late.

Abraham was drawn to God—right from the start. It was Abraham's love for the Lord that kept everything in perspective. Augustine once said, "Love God and do as you please." That sounds like a crazy statement. Do as you please? Really? Yes . . . if you truly love God as you ought to love God, you will want to do what pleases Him. Abraham understood that. He had his focus on eternal things. He was looking for the heavenly country and the city that is to come.

When the time came for Abraham and his nephew to part company, the older man said, "Let's try to part as friends." Abraham was a peacemaker. He said, "Listen, Lot. You choose what you want and where you want to go. If you want to go to the left, I'll go to the right. If you go to the right, I'll take the left. You decide." As he said in Genesis 13:9, "Is not the whole land before you? Please separate from me."

Abraham knew very well what he was doing. He was giving Lot the first and best choice. He could have said, "I'm in charge here, and I get the right to make my claim first." Instead, he decided to leave the outcome in the hands of God.

Lot made his choice, and in later years, he probably regretted it a million times over. Abraham chose to follow God no matter what, and ultimately, there are no regrets when you travel that road.

Are you in a similar situation right now? Maybe you're wondering if you can be totally honest and forthright in your business dealings. If you stay on the high road, you're afraid that lying cheat of a competitor will take advantage of you and steal away your profits. It would be easier to cut some corners and do a little cheating yourself. Here is the question you need to ask yourself. Are you more concerned with a fast buck or the approval of God?

Maybe you want to tell some of your friends about the Lord, but you're afraid it will cause some friction between you. You might even lose their friendship. Yes, and that's just what the Lord Jesus said might happen. Remember His words in Matthew 10:34–36? "Don't imagine that I came to bring peace to the earth! I came not to bring peace, but a sword. 'I have come to set a man against his father, a daughter against her mother, and a daughter-in-law against her mother-in-law. Your enemies will be right in your own household!'" (NLT).

The very friction you are dreading may be the catalyst that brings conversion to the life of your friend or family member. Most of us don't like conflict and would prefer to always get along with everybody. But if we take a stand for Jesus Christ, there will be people who don't like it and will oppose us. It just comes with the territory—as Jesus said it would. So here's how it boils down: Do you want harmony with people and friction with God or harmony with God and friction with people?

When I say friction I don't mean that you're acting mean or coming across heavy-handed. What I mean is that, humbly and graciously, you make your stand for truth and unashamedly own the name of Jesus. If that causes some temporary tension with someone, it is probably because that person is under the conviction of the Holy Spirit. All the while, tension or no tension, you will be praying for them to come to their senses and escape the snares of the evil one. Then, after they have come to Christ, you will enjoy ultimate unity and the real peace God wants to bring into your relationships.

Mistake after Mistake after Mistake

We have choices to make in life. Lot made a series of wrong steps that led to bigger and even worse choices. He ended up in a very dark place—somewhere he could have never imagined himself in his worst nightmare. That's the way it is with sin. Little things inevitably morph into bigger things.

Falling into sin is a lot like gaining weight. You say, "I don't want to get heavier. I want the scale to go left, not right." You try for a while, but then you cheat. You go to Taco Bell with your husband late at night, and order what he's having—a burrito supreme. If that's not bad enough, you follow him over to In-N-Out Burger and order your burger double-double-animal-style with chopped peppers.

In addition to heartburn, you notice that you are not able to button your jeans.

You say to yourself, "I've already messed up. I might as well get a large stack of pancakes for breakfast. I might as well keep messing up because I'm so far off my diet." And that is how sin works. We think, "I will do this little sin. I know I shouldn't do it, but I will do it once. Then I will do the other thing, and I might as well do the next thing, too, because I'm already way off course anyway." Little things turn into big things, and that is exactly what happened with Lot.

How did he end up in one of the worst, most God-hating cities on earth, Sodom? I think the progression went something like this.

Lot Looked the Wrong Way

In Genesis 13:10 we read, "And Lot lifted his eyes and saw all the plain of Jordan, that it was well watered everywhere (before the LORD destroyed Sodom and Gomorrah) like the garden of the LORD, like the land of Egypt as you go toward Zoar."

Notice that Lot's point of reference was Egypt. Why was he so drawn to Sodom? Because Sodom reminded him of the land where Abraham and the family had gone on one of their detours. Lot looked around, saw Sodom and Gomorrah on that wide, green plain, and took the first step down. By the way, this wasn't a casual glance. It appears it was a wistful look of longing.

Tony Bennett sang about "Leaving his heart in San Francisco." Apparently, Lot left his heart in Sodom.

Have you ever looked with longing at anything? Inside you are thinking, *I want that.* That car on the showroom floor. That outfit in the window. That hot doughnut coming down the conveyor belt at Krispy Kreme. That attractive girl or guy. All the trouble that would bring such tragedy to Lot's life began with a simple look—and an unfettered longing in his heart.

This is also what happened to Eve in the garden of Eden. She knew very well that she shouldn't eat from the forbidden tree, but thought, *What's the harm in taking a look?* In taking that look, she got very, very close to that tree, striking up a conversation with a serpent who "happened" to be hovering around the area. As Scripture says, she "*saw* that the tree was good for food, that it was pleasant to the eyes, and a tree desirable to make one wise" (Gen. 3:6, emphasis mine). She looked longingly at that beautiful fruit, and before she knew it, she was putting it into her mouth.

How different life would have been for Lot if, instead of lifting his eyes to the plain of Jordan, he had lifted his eyes to Heaven instead! What if he had asked God, the God of his Uncle Abraham, for direction? Instead, he looked toward Egypt—the wrong way.

The eye sees what the heart loves. Abraham took Lot out of Egypt, but apparently he couldn't get Egypt out of Lot. Remember this—outlook determines outcome.

Abraham walked by faith. That's what world changers do. Lot walked by sight.

Lot Separated Himself from Godly Influence

Abraham might have enjoyed putting distance between himself and his nephew, but it wasn't good for Lot. Cut loose from his uncle's positive influence and godly priorities, Lot drifted like a boat without moorings.

A sure sign of spiritual decline is when we find ourselves wanting to get away from people who love the Lord and walk with Him. If you find yourself restless and bored around Christians, that's not a good sign. When your wife says to you, "Honey, it's time for church," and you say, "Ugh," that is not a good sign. But it is a good sign when you are the one saying, "I've got the car ready, let's go to church. I can't wait to get there."

Are there people in your life who love the Lord and live for Him? Invite them out to lunch. Spend time with them and learn from them. If you don't know people like that, find them. A good church that teaches the Bible and honors Christ is a great place to start.

Lot Moved His Tents toward Sodom

Genesis 13:12 tells us that "Lot moved his tents to a place near Sodom" (NLT). Fascinated by the freewheeling lifestyle of these plains-dwellers and their disregard for God, Lot edged even closer to them, probably reasoning, "I can handle this." (That's what the chicken said when he moved into a duplex with the fox.)

What if you had the chance to talk to Lot after he'd moved his tent closer to the gates of Sodom? Imagine having a conversation with him, saying, "Hey Lot, what are you doing? Why are you moving closer to that wicked city?"

He might have replied, "I don't approve of what they do over there, but there are a lot of opportunities. I could go in there and influence people—maybe do some good."

"Yes, Lot, but then again . . . it might work the other way around."

It wasn't very long until Lot had moved from being *near* Sodom, into a condo with a long-term lease in the heart of the city.

It's a huge warning sign for all of us. If we try to get cozy with sin, to move just a little bit closer to the edge, we put ourselves in spiritual danger. Sometimes, God will send us warning signals. *That relationship with your coworker—you need to back off now, while you still can. That habit you have of stretching the truth—telling lies to cover up previous lies you've already told—you need to stop before it consumes you.* If we aren't alert and awake and seeking the Lord's daily protection, any one of us could end up like Lot.

Lot Went from the Frying Pan into the Fire

In Genesis 19:1, the Bible tells us that "Lot was sitting in the gate of Sodom."

We could very easily miss the implications of this verse. To be in the gateway meant that you were in a place of leadership. In effect, Lot got himself elected to the Sodom City Council. Leaders would gather at the city gate—a headquarters for local officials. Lot might have started out thinking he could influence them and reform Sodom just a little. (Which would be like rearranging deck chairs on the *Titanic*.) It wasn't long before Sodom swallowed up Lot and his whole family.

As I said before, Lot was more like a thermometer than a thermostat. He would end up simply reflecting whatever environment he was in. When he was with Abraham, he probably talked about God and pleasing Him. He would say,

"Amen," and "Praise the Lord." But when he was in Sodom, he didn't act like Abraham at all. Uncle Abe was the thermostat, changing the temperature wherever he went and bringing the Lord into all that he did. Lot was the thermometer, allowing Sodom's wickedness to infiltrate his thoughts and actions.

Jesus clearly told us that we are to be both salt and light—the salt of the earth and the light of the world. Some are salt but they're not light. What does that mean? They live the life, but they don't proclaim it. Others are light but not salt. They proclaim the life, but they don't live it. Yes, it is better to live it and not proclaim it than to proclaim it but not live it. Better yet, live the life *and* proclaim it.

Lot wasn't doing either one. He was the prototype of a compromising believer. Let's go back to the apostle Peter's commentary on Lot: "That good man Lot, driven nearly out of his mind by the sexual filth and perversity, was rescued. Surrounded by moral rot day after day after day, that righteous man was in constant torment. So God knows how to rescue the godly from evil trials" (2 Pet. 2:7–9 MSG).

So there he was in this incredibly wicked place, surrounded by all kinds of perversion. But no one made Lot move there, and no one was holding a gun to his head to keep him there. He could have walked away at any time. But he chose to stay.

Truth and Consequences

You can read the terrible consequences of Lot's decision to part with his uncle and live on the wild side in Genesis 19. It's not a pretty story.

When the two angels came to pull Lot and his family out of Sodom before God destroyed it, Lot's prospective sons-in-law didn't believe a word of it. They laughed in his face and said they would stay in Sodom. Lot's wife, after being warned not to look back when the destruction began, did look back—with longing and regret—and became a pillar of salt. When Lot found refuge in a cave, his two daughters, deeply influenced by the morals and attitudes of Sodom, got their dad drunk and had sex with him. Each girl conceived, and the children born to them became the nations of Ammon and Moab—implacable enemies of God's people for generations to come.

Meanwhile Abraham made the right choices, and after Lot had departed for greener pastures, the Lord took him aside and kindly confirmed that Abraham had done well. In Genesis 13:14–17 we read:

> Lift your eyes now and look from the place where you are—northward, southward, eastward, and westward; for all the land which you see I give to you and your descendants forever. And I will make your descendants as the dust of the earth; so that if a man could number the dust of the earth, then your descendants also could be numbered. Arise, walk in the land through its length and its width, for I give it to you.

Lot lifted up his eyes to see what the world had to offer. God invited Abraham to lift up his eyes and see what Heaven had to offer. Abraham offered Lot the best land. But God gave to Abraham the entire land. He would have it all—and Heaven just over the horizon. God always gives His very best to those that leave the choice with Him. To those who say, "Not my will but Yours be done."

One day when Jesus was with His disciples, they were talking about how much they had given up to follow Him, and Peter (it would be Peter) blurted out, "We've given up everything to follow you. What will we get?" (Matt. 19:27 NLT).

Jesus wasn't put off by Peter's question. Looking His disciples in the eyes, He made this amazing statement: "Everyone who has given up houses or brothers or sisters or father or mother or children or property, for my sake, will receive a hundred times as much in return and will inherit eternal life" (Matt. 19:29 NLT).

What have you given up to follow Jesus? Maybe you have given up some of the pleasures of this world. Maybe you have had to let go of relationships with old friends who were dragging you down. Maybe you have given up vices or addictions. Maybe you have given up some career plans. In effect, here is what God says to us. "I will make it up to you in this life, and especially in the life to come. You have My word on that." This is God's trade-in deal, and no one on earth can beat it.

Don't ever be afraid to commit an unknown future to a known God. Don't ever be afraid to say to the Lord, "You choose for me." God's choices for us will be far, far better than any choices we make for ourselves. The fact is, we really don't have all the information. We don't see everything. We just see the little moment that we are in. It's like looking through a quarter-inch slat in a high wood fence, and trying to make sense of a big, wide world. God sees horizon to horizon in our brief lives and, in His unfailing love, knows what is best.

You can trust your choices to Him.

The Temptations of a World Changer

How can I do such a wicked thing as this?
It would be a great sin against God.

~Genesis 39:9 TLB

I heard a story about a guy who loved Krispy Kreme doughnuts. The gold standard of doughnuts, in my opinion.

Every day on his way to work he made a stop at his local Krispy Kreme. But then, as you might expect, he found himself putting on unwanted pounds, and the clothing in his closet began to mysteriously shrink.

He really wanted to get back into fighting trim, so he put himself on a diet. To maintain that diet, he made a determination that he would not take his normal route to work, which passed right by the doughnut shop. He would take a different route to the office. In the long run, the extra ten minutes of drive time would be worth it.

All went well for a week and a half. Then one morning when he was preoccupied with something, he absentmindedly took the old way to work. And there was Krispy Kreme, gleaming in the morning sunlight. Worse yet, the neon, hot light sign was lit up in the window! That meant they were making fresh doughnuts—hot, fragrant, glazed doughnuts that would be rolling off the conveyor belt at any moment.

His thoughts went something like this. *Maybe this is a sign from God. Maybe I've been too hard on myself. Maybe the Lord wants me to have a Krispy Kreme doughnut.*

But there's always so much traffic around that place—especially when the sign is lit. So the man prayed. "Lord, if there is a parking space right in front, I will know this is from You."

The eighth time around the block a parking spot opened up.

It's good to make up your mind to resist temptation. And it is even better when you follow that up with a determination to stay far away from the sources of temptation. If you can avoid it, don't drive down a road where you know temptation waits.

Joseph was a world changer who faced some heavy-duty temptation he simply couldn't avoid. In this chapter, we will see how he handled himself when the same strong, in-your-face allurement hammered him day after day after day.

Maybe you're reading these words and saying to yourself, *I can't even remember the last time I was tempted.* That isn't necessarily a good thing. It may be that Satan leaves you alone because he doesn't perceive you as a threat. The devil looks at you and says, "Why bother?"

Then again, maybe you are thinking, *I get tempted all the time. I have these unwanted thoughts that hit me like incoming missiles. I really feel pushed around sometimes. Does that mean I'm not very spiritual?*

No, it doesn't. On the contrary, it could be an indication that you are on Satan's radar—that you are getting in his way and he sees you as an impediment to what he wants to accomplish. That may be why he has set his sights on you.

You might be surprised to know that testing and temptation can have a positive effect on the life of the believer. No one likes taking hits from hell or dealing with troubles and trials, but God can and will use them—for His kingdom and for our own good. Here is how the apostle James put it.

> When all kinds of trials and temptations crowd into your lives my brothers, don't resent them as intruders, but welcome them as friends! Realise that they come to test your faith and to produce in you the quality of endurance. But let the process go on until that endurance is fully developed, and you will find you have become men of mature character with the right sort of independence. (1:2–4 Phillips)

Joseph's story is an excellent example.

Out of the Frying Pan

The story of Joseph, covering twelve chapters in the book of Genesis, is one of the greatest stories in Scripture—or anywhere else. His appearance in the Hebrews 11 Hall of Faith is brief—essentially giving us a snapshot from the end of his life.

It was by faith that Joseph, when he was about to die, said confidently that the people of Israel would leave Egypt. He even commanded them to take his bones with them when they left. (Heb. 11:22 NLT)

The author of Hebrews could have said much, much more—but he probably figured his audience already knew Joseph's incredible story by heart. Joseph was a son of Abraham's grandson, Jacob, who had twelve sons born from four mothers. Because Joseph was the son of Rachel, Jacob's first love who later died in childbirth, Joseph was favored right from the beginning. As a result, his brothers hated him intensely and couldn't even speak a kind word to him.

Jacob must have been oblivious to this hatred and envy under his own roof, or he might never have sent seventeen-year-old Joseph by himself on a long journey to find his brothers and check up on them. When he finally located them, pasturing their sheep on an open range, they saw him coming from a distance and plotted to kill him and throw him into a pit. One of the brothers, however, objected to the murder and said they should sell him as a slave to a passing caravan. He probably figured they could at least make a little profit out of the deal. And that is just what they did.

This must have been the lowest point in young Joseph's life. Other dark times and trials would come in later years, but this must have been the worst.

What happened afterwards? "They put cruel chains on his ankles, an iron collar around his neck" (Ps. 105:18 MSG). And that is the way he had to walk from Israel to Egypt. He had to have been a mass of blisters and bruises when he finally arrived. But the bruises to his heart must have been even deeper. Sold as a slave! By his brothers! They hated him that much. And would he ever see his dad again?

The story picks up in Genesis 39, when Joseph arrived in Egypt.

> When Joseph was taken to Egypt by the Ishmaelite traders, he was purchased by Potiphar, an Egyptian officer. Potiphar was captain of the guard for Pharaoh, the king of Egypt. The LORD was with Joseph, so he succeeded in everything he did as he served in the home of his Egyptian master. Potiphar noticed this and realized that the LORD was with Joseph, giving him success in everything he did. This pleased Potiphar, so he soon made Joseph his personal attendant. He put him in charge of his entire household and everything he owned. From the day Joseph was put in charge of his master's household and property, the LORD began to bless Potiphar's household for Joseph's sake. All his household affairs ran smoothly, and his crops and livestock flourished. So Potiphar gave Joseph complete administrative responsibility over everything he owned. With Joseph there, he didn't worry about a thing—except what kind of food to eat! (vv. 1–6 NLT)

Joseph's world had completely changed in a very short time, through no fault of his own. But that's the way life on earth can be. You get a report from your doctor or a phone call in the night or an unexpected email that suddenly throws your peaceful world into chaos. With all your heart, you want to go back to the way things were—to those happy scenes in the rearview mirror. But life has changed, and you have to face it.

Joseph was now a slave in Egypt. He didn't like any part of that change. But one thing had stayed the same. The Bible says that the Lord was with Joseph. And that made all the difference in the world.

Egypt was a godless place—a pagan nation filled with religious superstition. The Egyptians at that time had up to two thousand gods and goddesses. How did they keep track of them all? I have trouble just remembering a few birthdays. They worshiped animals, insects, the Nile River, and Pharaoh himself. They were also given over to gross immorality. In massive building projects, they would utilize slave labor and even their own citizens.

To this teeming metropolis, this city of wickedness and idolatry, along came Joseph, a seventeen-year-old Hebrew boy who had led a sheltered, privileged life. It was the classic story of a country boy being dropped into the middle of the big city. But Joseph wasn't there as a young tourist with a backpack and a few reservations at some youth hostels. Joseph was a slave who was placed on the auction block for sale to the highest bidder.

He was purchased by a man named Potiphar, identified in Genesis 39:1 as captain of the guard for Pharaoh. You might say that Potiphar headed up the military police and was also a royal bodyguard—the Secret Service of his day. Some say that Potiphar was also chief executioner. In other words, everyone put to death was done so by order of Potiphar. I'm not sure what his name meant in Egyptian; it probably translated to *onebadadudo*. One bad dude.

As we read the biblical account, however, we don't find Joseph cowering in some corner, moaning, "Don't beat me, master!" Not at all. Joseph, who had every reason to be intimidated by his circumstances, wasn't intimidated at all. Why? Genesis 39:2 has the answer: "The Lord was with Joseph."

The God of Abraham, Isaac, and Jacob was Joseph's strength and confidence in the midst of a frightening reality.

Prosperity inside Adversity

By the way, the very same Lord is with you too! You know that, don't you? If you are a Christian, He is with you. In Hebrews 13:5–6, the Lord says to us, "Never will I leave you; never will I forsake you." And in return, "We say with confidence, 'The Lord is my helper; I will not be afraid. What can mere mortals do to me?'" (NIV)

That's a cause for courage and confidence, even in the face of great trials and changes in your life.

The prophet Elijah was able to walk courageously into the court of Ahab and his wicked wife, Jezebel, and speak the words God gave him. Elijah recognized he was standing before God wherever he went, and Joseph understood the same.

Joseph was a classic example of the first three verses in Psalm 1:

> Blessed is the man
> Who walks not in the counsel of the ungodly,
> Nor stands in the path of sinners,
> Nor sits in the seat of the scornful;
> But his delight is in the law of the LORD,
> And in His law he meditates day and night.
> He shall be like a tree
> Planted by the rivers of water,
> That brings forth its fruit in its season,
> Whose leaf also shall not wither;
> And whatever he does shall prosper.

Take another look at those last two lines.

God does want to prosper His people. But here's the problem. There is a group of contemporary Christians who subscribe to something called "the prosperity gospel." They have taken a basic truth from Scripture and so emphasized and exaggerated it that pastors are afraid to even talk about God-given prosperity anymore. The prosperity gospel makes the unbiblical claim that God wants everyone to be healthy and wealthy all the time, with no sickness or suffering intruding into our lives.

Joseph certainly prospered, yes. But that prosperity also included false accusations, disappointments, significant jail time, and being torn from home and family. Even in God's prosperity, there can be hardship, but ultimately God wants to bless us and restore us, as He did with Joseph.

Stay Faithful in the Routine

You might say that Joseph was a model of how a Christian should function in the workplace. Potiphar was undoubtedly a hard and demanding guy to work for, but Joseph went about his tasks with diligence, wisdom, and integrity. Colossians 3:22–25 gives us direction about how we should pursue our jobs each day:

> Servants, do what you're told by your earthly masters. And don't just do the minimum that will get you by. Do your best. Work from the heart for your real Master, for God, confident that you'll get paid in full when you come into your inheritance. Keep in mind always that the ultimate Master you're serving is Christ. The sullen servant who does shoddy work

will be held responsible. Being a follower of Jesus doesn't cover up bad work. (MSG)

You want to be a good witness and a good worker before anything else. That earns you the right to share your faith, when the right moment arrives. But if you consistently clock out early and you're not a responsible worker, no one will pay attention to your words about Christ. On the other hand, if you work with integrity realizing that your ultimate boss is the Lord Himself, and not the man or woman who signs your paycheck, it will change everything around you.

Joseph underwent severe testing. Maybe you are being tested right now. You might be working somewhere in obscurity, maybe in an entry-level job making minimum wage. You may be washing dishes, bussing tables, framing houses, or flipping burgers. Here is what will make all the difference. *Do it for the Lord. Do it to please Him.* Wash dishes for Him. Make that hamburger as if the Lord Himself were pulling up to the drive-through and rolling down His window. It will change the way you see work when you get up in the morning.

That is how Joseph saw it, and the Lord made him successful. Everyone noticed the excellence of his work and his attitude, including Egypt's top cop, Potiphar. He was so successful that Potiphar made him his executive assistant, essentially second in command over the household. A teenage, foreign slave with power over an Egyptian home! How amazing is that?

Before long, Potiphar was saying, "Listen, son, I'm putting you over the books in the house. You manage the money and pay the bills. Here are the passwords to all my accounts and my American Express Platinum card. You are in charge of the house. In fact, all I am worrying about today is what to have for lunch—unless you have suggestions about that too."

That may seem great, but sometimes when things are going well, we become more vulnerable to temptation. When we're dealing with pain or can't make ends meet or have some big problem we're wrestling with, we rightly become very dependent upon God. We say, "Oh God, please help me!" But then when things are going well, when we have a little extra money in the bank, when we're having a run of great health or maybe seeing fruit in our ministry, we can become a little complacent, a little less likely to seek the Lord every day.

That is when temptation will hit, and that's when it hit Joseph.

And that's when it hit King David too.

When we look back on David's life in the Bible, we typically associate two names with his—two names that say it all. When we say, "David and Goliath," we remember David's greatest victory—the day he shouted defiance at a blasphemous Philistine giant and took him down with a sling and a stone. But when we say, "David and Bathsheba," we think of David's greatest shame and worst defeat.

When did that defeat occur? When did David fall into sin with Bathsheba? It happened after he had been successful and ruled for many years. He was kicking back one night and taking a break from all his kingly duties. He was also on a dangerous spiritual vacation. And in this moment of idleness, in the afterglow of much success, temptation blew up in his face like a roadside IED, knocking him flat, changing the trajectory of his life, and breaking many hearts.

Joseph, however, was more on his guard than David had been. Here is what happened when temptation suddenly confronted Joseph in the midst of his duties.

> Joseph was a very handsome and well-built young man, and Potiphar's wife soon began to look at him lustfully. "Come and sleep with me," she demanded.
>
> But Joseph refused. "Look," he told her, "my master trusts me with everything in his entire household. No one here has more authority than I do. He has held back nothing from me except you, because you are his wife. How could I do such a wicked thing? It would be a great sin against God."
>
> She kept putting pressure on Joseph day after day, but he refused to sleep with her, and he kept out of her way as much as possible. One day, however, no one else was around when he went in to do his work. She came and grabbed him by his cloak, demanding, "Come on, sleep with me!" Joseph tore himself away, but he left his cloak in her hand as he ran from the house. (Gen. 39:6–12 NLT)

Do you remember that old saying? "Hell hath no fury like a woman scorned." Mrs. Potiphar felt scorned big time by this upstart slave. She was so angry at him for rejecting her advances and demands that she falsely accused him of attempted rape. She yelled to Joseph's fellow servants, "Look what this man did! He tried to take advantage of me, but when I screamed, he left his coat behind and ran!" (see Gen. 39:18). And then when her husband got home, she told him the same story.

Did Potiphar believe her? I don't believe he did. As Egypt's top cop, he probably knew a phony story and false testimony when he heard it. I imagine that he knew his wife was a liar and a seductress, who had made the whole thing up. But he probably had to follow through and punish Joseph as an example to the rest of the household. If he had really believed her story, Joseph would have lost his head within the hour.

Mrs. Potiphar was the original cougar; she wanted Joseph to be her boy toy. By the way, Joseph was a single man in his twenties, with all his normal God-given sexual desires running at full steam. What's more, he had been in Egypt ten years, surrounded by the godless, immoral values of that land. And there's no doubt that the lady of the house pulled out all the stops to look seductive and alluring. Joseph could have thought, *Who would ever know? Maybe it would help my career. Besides, what happens in Egypt stays in Egypt, right?*

But he didn't do that, did he? He stayed faithful to the Lord, even though his troubles got much worse.

Stay Away When You Can

I love Genesis 39:10: "He kept out of her way as much as possible" (NLT).

That was a good strategy! One of the best ways to deal with temptation is to steer clear of obvious dangers and traps however we can. Granted, temptation can hit us anywhere—even sitting in church. It could be an immoral thought—or anger, hatred, or jealousy. It can confront us at any time and in any place.

But let's all be honest. We know very well there are places and times when we are more vulnerable. Remember the guy who had a thing for Krispy Kreme doughnuts? He knew if he drove by and saw the neon sign lit up, he would end up going in. We know where we are weak, and so does our adversary, the devil.

Satan is no amateur at this temptation business, and he knows how to set an attractive trap. He won't tell you the truth about his intentions. He won't say, "Hey, you happy Christian. Follow my lead here and let me ruin your life. I want to destroy your family—including your kids, your grandkids, and your great-grandkids who aren't even born yet. I'd like to see you become an addict or an alcoholic. Maybe if things go well from my perspective, somewhere down the road you will be in such despair that you will take your own life. What do you think? Do you still want to get in this taxi with me and go for a ride?"

What moron would respond to a come-on like that?

But the devil is smarter than that. His line of reasoning will probably sound more like this: "I know you would never be unfaithful to your spouse. I know you would never lie or steal. I'm just talking about a little harmless flirting here. Just for fun. Just try this thing out. Take a little taste. Take a test drive. Just try it on once. Take this thought out for a spin."

That is where the problems begin. It starts with something very small and seemingly insignificant. A little pebble rolling down a slope . . . that launches a landslide carrying away a hillside. Theologian Martin Luther once said, "You cannot keep birds from flying over your head, but you can keep them from building a nest in your hair."[1] Now in my case, the bird had better bring his own materials because there isn't much to work with on my head. Even so, it's a good word picture.

If the devil knocks on your door, don't invite him in for tea. Don't even answer the knock. Just leave the door closed and double locked. The apostle James says, "Humble yourselves before God. Resist the devil, and he will flee from you" (4:7 NLT).

That is what Joseph did. To the best of his ability, he kept out of Mrs. Potiphar's way.

But the woman was relentless. She kept the pressure on Joseph again and again. I am sure she used every verbal and visual seduction technique she could think of. But in spite of her persistence, in spite of his natural desires and tendencies, in spite of the advancement it could have given his career, in spite of his own miserable background at home, he resisted.

How did he do it? Verse 9 gives us the answer. He basically said, "How could I do such a wicked thing? It would be a great sin against God." With God's help, Joseph was able to see the big picture of his life, and that kept him from caving in to a few moments of sensual pleasure.

So how do we overcome temptation? Here are a few takeaway points to help you face temptation and come out victorious.

Everyone Will Be Tempted

Temptation is not a sin. In fact, it is a call to battle. As I said earlier, it might even be an indication that your life is on course, and that you are moving in the right direction.

Jesus Himself was tempted at the beginning and the end of His ministry. Right after He was baptized by his Cousin John in the Jordan River, the Father spoke and said, "This is My beloved Son, in whom I am well pleased" (Matt 3:17).

What happened after that? The Bible says, "Immediately the Spirit drove Him into the wilderness. And He was there in the wilderness forty days, tempted by Satan, and was with the wild beasts" (Mark 1:12–13).

Immediately. Right away. He was drilled with temptation after temptation at the very launch of His ministry on earth. Before that ordeal was complete, the devil said to Jesus, in effect, "Worship me right now and you don't even have to go to the cross. Here are all the kingdoms of the world and their glory—from the first century into eternity. I will give it all to You on a silver platter if You will worship me. Worship me and it will all be Yours."

Jesus resisted that temptation to avoid the cross, but it would come again at the very end of His life. Hanging on a Roman cross with nails through His hands and feet, Jesus had to listen to His enemies mocking Him and laughing at Him. "Aha! You who destroy the temple and build it in three days, save Yourself, and come down from the cross!" (Mark 15:29–30). "He saved others; let Him save Himself if He is the Christ, the chosen of God" (Luke 23:35).

And He could have done just that. He certainly could have saved Himself. As Jesus told Peter in Gethsemane, He could have called twelve legions of angels to rescue Him and obliterate His enemies. Thank God He didn't, or you and I would be lost beyond hope.

If Jesus faced temptation at the beginning and end of His ministry, should we expect that it will be any different for you and me?

I heard about an old pastor who was asked by a young man, "Pastor, when I get older, will the temptations finally stop?" The older man wisely replied, "I wouldn't trust myself until I had been dead for three days." There is no escaping temptation this side of Heaven.

Sin Has Consequences

In one of their tense confrontations, Joseph told Mrs. Potiphar, "Look . . . my master trusts me with everything in his entire household. No one here has more authority than I do. He has held back nothing from me except you, because you are his wife" (Gen. 39:8–9 NLT).

I find Joseph's reasoning here interesting. Potiphar was a slave owner who had purchased Joseph. Yet Joseph showed loyalty to him. He was saying, in effect, "Your husband has been good to me and given me some incredible opportunities. I wouldn't do that to him."

Joseph may have also been thinking about his reputation, and how it reflected on the God of Israel. He was a Hebrew man who believed in the one true God, rather than the menagerie of Egyptian deities.

I just wish people would think a little bit before plunging into a sin that will destroy multiple lives. At some point, before someone enters into an affair, they have to contemplate it. They have to think it over. That very word *affair* sounds lighthearted and fun, like going on a cruise. Better to call it what it is: Adultery. Sexual sin. Hell on wheels.

What if people took a minute or two to consider the repercussions, before diving headlong into something so far-reaching and life-changing. How will it affect your spouse? What impact will it have on your children? How will it hit your parents when they hear the news? And what about the person you're involved with? How will it change the trajectory of his or her life and for generations afterward?

People don't think about those things. We're too busy thinking of ourselves and our desires. I've heard people justify sexual sin by saying, "My marriage isn't fulfilling anymore. This new person in my life understands me like nobody else. We're soul mates. I am going to divorce my spouse, marry this person, and start a new life. Then I will be happy."

Actually, the statistics are against you. I recently read *Affair-Proof Your Marriage: Understanding, Preventing and Surviving an Affair* by Lana Staheli, and it included some interesting numbers on marriage. In her book, Staheli tells readers that 80 percent of those who break up their marriage to marry someone else are sorry later. Of those who do marry their lover, which is only about 10 percent, 70 percent of them get a divorce. And of that 25 to 30 percent that stay married, only half of them are happy.

Think about that. Our sins have consequences, and they are horrific.

Young and virile and vulnerable as Joseph may have been, he *did* think about the consequences of his actions, and God gave him the strength not to shipwreck his young life.

Let the Bible Guide You—Even in Confusing Times

God's standards don't change. Yes, Scripture clearly describes Joseph's dysfunctional home and rough childhood. He had hateful, vindictive brothers. He'd been snatched from his homeland and dropped in an utterly foreign and alien environment. And he was living in a pagan culture saturated by pagan morals.

So much had changed for him. But some things don't change. God's Word does not change. Even if culture changes, God's Word stands firm. A lot of people would have told Joseph, "Hey, go for it if you can get away with it. Slavery should have some compensations!" But Joseph knew it was wrong. He knew it was a sin against his God. The price of a few moments of pleasure was far, far too high.

We live in a time when wrong is perceived as right, and right is perceived as wrong. You might say, "This is okay because I'm single and lonely." Or maybe, "My marriage isn't working. My needs aren't being met." Maybe so. But wrong is wrong even if you don't get caught. Wrong is wrong even if others are doing things far worse. *Wrong is wrong even if it doesn't bother your conscience.*

Sometimes people's hearts get hardened. The Bible talks about people who have had their conscience seared as with a hot iron (see 1 Tim. 4:2).

I have a super powerful iron at home that was made in Europe. It has a steam-blast mechanism that works better than any American iron I've ever had. I fill up the tank with water, and I iron stuff with blasts of superhot steam. Not long ago I noticed the shirt I was wearing had a wrinkle creasing the front, but I was in a bit of a hurry. A normal, rational person would take the shirt off and iron it. But I thought, *I'll save a little time here by ironing it while it's still on. I'll give it a blast of steam.*

I held the iron out in front of me at arms-length and gave it a blast. When it hit me I screamed like a little girl. It was so painful. But the wrinkle was gone! That night as I was getting ready for bed, my wife looked at me and said, "What's that? What's that big red welt on your chest?"

And I said, "Don't ask."

Our hearts can get like that. They can be seared. The literal meaning is "cauterized," meaning you no longer feel or sense what you used to.

I remember spending time with Billy Graham at a Crusade in Portland, Oregon. I don't remember what the sermon was about, but I will always remember one line. He told the thousands gathered there that night that "Christ can re-sensitize your conscience." That's wonderful to know, but you shouldn't always let your conscience be your guide. (Apologies to Jiminy Cricket.) Your conscience can mislead you! In the book of Jeremiah, the Lord says, "The heart is deceitful above all things and beyond cure. Who can understand it?" (17:9 NIV).

You should let the Bible be your guide. This is the one absolute you can always stand on and be certain of.

Avoid the Things That Tempt You

Joseph understood this principle. I love what he said to Mrs. Potiphar when she tried to get him to sin: "How can I do this thing *and sin against God*?" That Egyptian woman didn't care a thing about God but Joseph did. He might not have had a written Bible to carry around, but he knew the stories about his father, Jacob, his grandfather, Isaac, and his great-grandfather, Abraham. He wasn't about to bring dishonor on the name of the God who had been so good to his family.

So he ran as fast as he could.

Genesis 39:12 actually tells us: "He ran from the house" (NLT). Sometimes that is the best way to deal with a strong temptation. Just get out of its clutches. Remove yourself from the situation, no matter how awkward that might seem at the moment.

Sometimes when I am counseling someone, the conversation will go like this.

"I keep getting tempted and falling into sin."

"Tell me about the last time this happened."

"I was tempted to have sex with my girlfriend."

"Okay, where were you?"

"In a hotel room."

"You were in a hotel room . . . with her?"

"Yes."

"And where were you in the room?"

"Lying on the bed."

I don't want to be overly harsh here, but that is simply stupid behavior. You can't expect God to deliver you from temptation after you have sent it an engraved invitation and welcomed it into your living room.

Someone else will say to me, "I'm having this struggle with drinking. I'm an alcoholic and I just fell off the wagon again."

"I didn't see you in church last Sunday, where were you?"

"At a bar."

"Why in the world would you hang out in a bar?"

"They have these amazing chicken wings and big TV screens. You can watch five sporting events at once."

You have got to stay away from those areas where you are vulnerable. You may think I'm being overly simplistic here but I'm not. The wisest man in the world told a similar story a few millennia ago.

> While I was at the window of my house,
>> looking through the curtain,
> I saw some naive young men,
>> and one in particular who lacked common sense.
> He was crossing the street near the house of an
>> immoral woman,

strolling down the path by her house.
It was at twilight, in the evening,
as deep darkness fell.
The woman approached him,
seductively dressed and sly of heart.
(Prov. 7:6–10 NLT)

Moral of the story? If you deliberately cross the street and stroll down the path of temptation in the dark of night, bad things will happen. Count on it.

Say Yes to God

When Joseph said no to Potiphar's wife on that fateful day, he was saying yes to God.

There is a blessing waiting for the man or woman who resists temptation. I know it is hard in the moment, when the pressure's on. It's not easy to say no. But here is the good news. The temptation will pass, and you will be blessed if you've overcome it. James 1:12 says, "Blessed is the man who endures temptation; for when he has been approved, he will receive the crown of life which the Lord has promised to those who love Him." And remember that the word *blessed* could just as easily be translated as "happy."

Joseph loved the Lord, and in the heat of temptation's flames, he said a firm no to his own passions and desires.

Maybe you are living in an ungodly place right now. You might be the only believer in your family—or the only Christian in your neighborhood. You put out a nativity scene in your front yard at Christmas and everyone looks at you like you're a lunatic. Or maybe you are the person the teacher will often make jokes about because of your faith in God. Or you are the only person who believes at your company. You know what it's like to be in a wicked place. You say, "Hey, this is hard. I'm surrounded by temptations day and night. How can I stay pure in a place like this?"

Talk to the Lord about it. Tell Him every detail every day. Keep putting the Word of God into your heart, mind, and memory. Look for those ways of escape the New Testament talks about (1 Cor. 10:13).

And then look forward to the very particular and especially wonderful individual blessings God will pour into your life in His time.

That's what Joseph did, and that's how he changed the world and used God's mighty strength to overcome temptation.

The World Changer
Who Faced a Giant

You come to me with sword, spear, and javelin, but
I come to you in the name of the LORD of Heaven's
Armies—the God of the armies of Israel, whom you
have defied.

~1 Samuel 17:45 NLT

We all face giants in life.

If you're not standing in the shadow of one right
now, you will. Giants come with the territory on planet
earth.

Jesus warned us that "In this world you will have trouble"
(John 16:33 NIV). And when that trouble grows and morphs
into an impossible situation or an insurmountable obstacle,
we might call it a giant.

A giant is something that brings fear into your life and seems to have you in its grip. It looms large and menacing and won't leave you alone—it's something dark and sinister that prowls the perimeters of your life. Maybe at times you seemed to overcome this giant, or sent it away for a week or two, thinking you were victorious. But then it came back with a vengeance—stronger, uglier, and more intimidating than ever.

It could be a giant of fear. Whenever you think about a certain situation in your life, you're gripped with anxiety and dread. It may not even be what people call a "rational fear," but so what? It's real to you, and that's bad enough. You find yourself asking, "What if this happens or what if that happens? What would I do? What *could* I do?"

Then again, maybe the giant is some personal sin or habit—an area where you are weak and keep falling over and over again. It could be pride, envy, gluttony, pornography, alcohol, drugs, or something else.

Your giant might be the threat of a real-life bully, a lawsuit, or someone attacking you or your business on social media, writing unkind things or outright lies.

Maybe the giant for you is worry over a nonbelieving loved one—a husband or wife or prodigal son or daughter. You've prayed and prayed, but they only seem to drift further from the truth.

Here is what you need to know—and this may be the very reason the Lord directed you to pick up this particular book in the first place—*you can overcome these giants.* We need to face our giants in faith and remember that God is bigger than any oversized adversary or towering obstacle we may be facing.

You may have guessed where I'm going with this chapter. I want to talk about a teenager named David and the day he unexpectedly found himself facing the biggest, most frightening, seemingly undefeatable challenge of his life.

Weakness Turned to Strength

David was clearly a world changer. Think about this. The nation of Israel lives today in its ancient homeland, and at the top of every flagpole a beautiful white banner with two horizontal blue lines and a blue star ripples in the breeze. That's the Star of David. And if you had a few extra bucks to spend on accommodations in Jerusalem, you could book yourself a night in the King David Hotel on King David Street. There is even a folk song they still sing in Israel today with the lyrics, "David is the King of Israel!"

David lived three thousand years ago. But his name is as relevant now as it was then. He also appears in our Hebrews 11 Hall of Faith.

> How much more do I need to say? It would take too long to recount the stories of the faith of Gideon, Barak, Samson, Jephthah, David, Samuel, and all the prophets. By faith these people overthrew kingdoms, ruled with justice, and received what God had promised them. They shut the mouths of lions, quenched the flames of fire, and escaped death by the edge of the sword. Their weakness was turned to strength. They became strong in battle and put whole armies to flight. (vv. 32–34 NLT)

David stopped the mouths of lions—literally! He was valiant in battle, escaped the edge of the sword, and caused great armies to flee. And on the day when he faced a nine-foot-six-inch freak of nature, his weakness was turned to strength.

David, the youngest son of a sheep rancher from Bethlehem named Jesse, was a study in contrasts. He was both a warrior and a worshiper. You've heard people say, "I'm a lover, not a fighter." David was both. He was also a general, a king, a poet, a gifted musician, and a sinner who broke God's heart. But when we first met him in Scripture, he was a shepherd boy watching over his dad's flocks.

Great events were transpiring in Israel as David led his sheep from pasture to pasture. The Lord had told Samuel, Israel's prophet and spiritual leader, that He was done with disobedient King Saul and wanted Samuel to anoint a new king to lead His people. God directed His prophet to the house of Jesse.

To the surprise of everyone in the village, the prophet rolled into town.

This was a very big deal. His very presence sent shock waves. He was a genuine, living, breathing prophet of God. The whole town turned out, all waiting to hear what the man of God had to say. Samuel offered a sacrifice to the Lord and asked the old rancher Jesse to introduce his boys.

Jesse had seven strapping sons and proudly paraded them before the visiting prophet. You might call them "the Magnificent Seven," because they were all strong and manly specimens. As Samuel walked along, looking at each one of them, he wondered which one the Lord had picked as the next king.

What he heard the Lord saying was, "Not that one, not that one, not that one"—right on through the lineup. Then Samuel stood in front of Eliab, the tallest and best looking of Jesse's sons. The prophet thought to himself, *This has to be the guy. I could see his face on postage stamps. It's like he came from central casting. This guy is kingly material if I've ever seen it.*

That's when the Lord nailed His servant with words that all of us should keep in mind: "Don't judge by his appearance or height, for I have rejected him. The LORD doesn't see things the way you see them. People judge by outward appearance, but the LORD looks at the heart" (1 Sam. 16:7 NLT).

So after checking out "the Magnificent Seven," Samuel learned that not one of them fit the bill. Looking back at Jesse, the prophet asked, "Do you have any more boys?" Almost reluctantly, the rancher replied, "There is still the youngest. . . . But he's out in the fields watching the sheep and goats."

"Send for him at once," Samuel said. "We will not sit down to eat until he arrives" (1 Sam. 16:11 NLT).

I wonder if Jesse wanted to warn Samuel off. I wonder if he wanted to say, "Yeah, there's one more, out in the back forty. But he's not the type you're looking for. He plays his little harp, sings to God, and practices half the day with his slingshot. He's a decent shepherd, but I don't know what else he's good for."

But Samuel said, "Bring him."

So young David came bounding in, bright-eyed, energetic, and ready for whatever.

With Jesse, the seven brothers, and half the town looking on with lowered jaws, Samuel anointed David's head with oil, indicating that he would be the next king of Israel. And then the prophet left town, and everyone was left scratching their heads. *David? Oil? King? What in the world just happened?*

This would have been especially strange for David. He must have wondered, *What am I supposed to do now?* With no better plan, he went back to the pasture and the family's sheep.

He would wait on the Lord, just as he had always waited on the Lord.[1]

Facing the Giant

Sometime later Israel was at war with their longtime enemy, the Philistines. On one side of the big valley of Elah were the Philistines and their army, and on the other side were the Israelites. With all of David's brothers on the front lines of the Israeli army, Jesse was concerned. There were no cell phones or news stations in those days, so he sent his youngest son, David, to the front lines to check on his brothers and bring them bread and cheese. Sounds like a pizza delivery to me.

When David arrived, he heard some overgrown freak of nature strutting around in armor and mocking Israel and Israel's God. That instantly made David's blood boil. Who was this ugly giant to mock the armies of the living God? Why weren't King Saul and his army doing something about this? When he began asking questions of the soldiers and officers, David's brother got angry at him, and put his little brother down.

"What are you doing around here anyway? . . . What about those few sheep you're supposed to be taking care of? I know about your pride and deceit. You just want to see the battle!" (1 Sam. 17:28 NLT).

David was used to this behavior. When you have seven older brothers, you learn to expect that kind of treatment. He shook off the sarcasm and kept asking questions.

Goliath had descended from a family of gigantic human beings, and he must have presented a terrifying sight. Over nine feet tall, solid muscle, and covered with state-of-the-art body armor, he was challenging someone—anyone—in Israel's army to take him on. The giant warrior had a giant sneer on his face. "Hey, I'll tell you what," he was saying. "We'll make this a two-person war. If your guy beats me, *mano a mano*, the Philistines will be your servants. But if I beat him (which I will), then you will be our servants. What do you say?"

In the meantime, David was looking around at Israel's soldiers, saying, "What's wrong with you guys? Why are you so intimidated? Are you going to let this big goon talk like that? He's mocking God! Why isn't somebody fighting him?"

The soldiers replied, "Are you crazy, kid? No one wants to step into the ring with a giant."

So David said, "Okay, I will fight him."

After they got up off the ground from laughing for twenty minutes, they were probably saying, "You? You and what army?"

"Never mind. I'll take care of it right now. Me and the Lord. I'll face him by faith. Let's go." With that, the young shepherd set out to tackle the giant. The Bible picks up this incredible story in 1 Samuel 17.

[David] picked up five smooth stones from a stream and put them into his shepherd's bag. Then, armed only with his shepherd's staff and sling, he started across the valley to fight the Philistine.

Goliath walked out toward David with his shield bearer ahead of him, sneering in contempt at this ruddy-faced boy. "Am I a dog," he roared at David, "that you come at me with a stick?" And he cursed David by the names of his gods. "Come over here, and I'll give your flesh to the birds and wild animals!" Goliath yelled.

David replied to the Philistine, "You come to me with sword, spear, and javelin, but I come to you in the name of the LORD of Heaven's Armies—the God of the armies of Israel, whom you have defied. Today the LORD will conquer you, and I will kill you and cut off your head. And then I will give the dead bodies of your men to the birds and wild animals, and the whole world will know that there is a God in Israel! And everyone assembled here will know that the LORD rescues his people, but not with sword and spear. This is the LORD's battle, and he will give you to us!"

As Goliath moved closer to attack, David quickly ran out to meet him. Reaching into his shepherd's bag and taking out a stone, he hurled it with his sling and hit the Philistine in the forehead. The stone sank in, and Goliath stumbled and fell face down on the ground.

So David triumphed over the Philistine with only a sling and a stone, for he had no sword. Then David ran over and pulled Goliath's sword from its sheath. David used it to kill him and cut off his head.

When the Philistines saw that their champion was dead, they turned and ran. (vv. 40–51 NLT)

What do we learn from this story about facing our own giants on our own private battlefields?

We All Face Giants in Life

Giants of some sort will come lumbering into everyone's life, making their threats and casting their shadows. We will all face severe hardships. We will all face seemingly insurmountable obstacles. We will all deal with temptation. So whatever you are wrestling with, whatever you may be going through right now, whatever giant you may hear bellowing threats into your world, you need to know this: You're not the only one. It's part of life on this side of Heaven.

If you are struggling with the "giant" of temptation, 1 Corinthians 10:13 reminds us that "the temptations in your life are no different from what others experience. And God is faithful. He will not allow the temptation to be more than you can stand. When you are tempted, he will show you a way out so that you can endure" (NLT).

It's true that we all face giants. But this is also true. *Every giant can be defeated.*

This big Philistine throwback may have been a giant, but he was also a human being. A man. And remember the words of Hebrews 13? "So we say with confidence, 'The Lord is my helper; I will not be afraid. What can mere mortals do to me?'" (v. 6 NIV).

Goliath started life like the rest of us—as a baby. Even so, he must have been one massive baby. I can imagine the conversation between his parents.

"It's time to change Goliath's diaper."

"I'm not doing that. I did it last time and I'm still traumatized. It's your turn."

Then the baby became a toddler. Can you imagine Goliath in his terrible twos? And over the course of time, he became an adolescent before maturing into a man. He started small and got very big.

That's the way it is with most giants in our lives. Little things turn into big things. Let's say you have a problem with drinking. Maybe it started out with just having a beer with the boys or a glass of wine with dinner. But then you decided you wanted a drink when you first got home from work to help you unwind. As time went by, you found you needed a drink to get you going in the morning—or a drink in the early afternoon to get you over the hump and make it through a difficult day. Then you found yourself unable to go through a day without a drink. You looked yourself in the mirror one morning and realized that you were a functioning alcoholic. It started so small. It was such a harmless pastime that helped you socially blend in with others. And then it became a giant with a club, and you couldn't escape.

As a pastor for almost fifty years, I've seen what alcohol does in people's lives. I've witnessed the destruction of marriages, families, and lives. Just recently, I heard about two pastors who actually had to leave their churches because they found themselves with out-of-control drinking problems. This is a giant we don't want to wink at. Our so-called liberty could very easily morph into a giant we can no longer control.

Maybe your giant pertains to your immediate family. You might have an unbelieving husband or wife or a prodigal child. You've shared the gospel with them, you've prayed for them. Maybe you've nagged and pressured them, but nothing has worked and you're about to give up hope that they will ever come to Christ. You have become weary in the battle. It's not easy dealing with a Goliath under your own roof! This is when we have to remember what David remembered, right from the start.

It's Not Our Battle

David knew the battle belonged to the Lord. Look again at verse 47 in a different translation: "Everyone gathered here will learn that GOD doesn't save by means of sword or spear. The battle belongs to GOD" (1 Sam. 17:47 MSG).

I'm reminded of another battle that occurred later in Israel's history. Jehoshaphat, a godly king of Judah in Jerusalem, faced a monstrous threat from three invading, converging armies. Judah's little army was hopelessly outmanned, outmaneuvered, and outgunned. Realizing this, Jehoshaphat cried out to the Lord in front of everybody, "O our God, will You not judge them? For we have no power against this great multitude that is coming against us; nor do we know what to do, but our eyes are upon You" (2 Chron. 20:12).

At that moment, a Spirit-filled man stood up in the assembly and with a loud voice called out, "Thus says the LORD to you: 'Do not be afraid nor dismayed because of this great multitude, for the battle is not yours, but God's'" (v. 15).

Our Strength Comes from the Lord

Why do giants intimidate and defeat us so often? Because when we try to face them in our own strength with our own meager resources, we find ourselves overwhelmed. Ephesians 6 tells us how to armor up for battle, with the helmet of salvation, the breastplate of righteousness, the shield of faith and so on. But before you do anything else, the passage says to "be strong in the Lord and in the power of His might" (v. 10).

You can't win spiritual battles or defeat giants in your own strength. You can only do it through trusting in God's power and resting in His strength. We fight fire with fire. What do I mean by that? We're in a spiritual battle so let's use the spiritual weapons God has given us.

Is something troubling you as you read these words? Do you find yourself with a situation tied up in so many knots that you can't imagine how to sort it out? Turn your worries into worship. Turn your fears into prayers. Turn your problems into petitions.

Scripture is so very, very clear on this. In Philippians 4:6–7, Paul tells us, "Don't worry about anything; instead, pray about everything. Tell God what you need, and thank him for all he has done. Then you will experience God's peace, which exceeds anything we can understand. His peace will guard your hearts and minds as you live in Christ Jesus" (NLT).

Wow, what a promise! So let's believe it and act on it in faith. Pray about that nonbelieving husband or wife or son or daughter. Get together with other Christian friends and pray together. And just watch how your perspective changes as you roll these heavy issues off your shoulders and onto the Lord's, where they belong.

Begin by acknowledging the One you are speaking to. This is your all-powerful, all-knowing, loving Father who created all worlds and is in charge of everything. When you see God for who He is, you will begin to see your problem for what it is. Sometimes our problems look like towering giants because our view of God is so small. But when we see them in the perspective of God's greatness, power, grace, and love, they resume their proper proportions.

Yes, David realized that Goliath was nine-foot-six in his bare feet and eye-level with a basketball hoop. But God is the One who formed the earth and scattered the stars. Nine-foot-six or *ninety*-foot-six isn't large to Him! There is no giant, no obstacle, no problem, and no situation that is too big for God to bring down.

Attack Your Giants

Early in the story we read that Goliath was actually coming up into the Israeli camp each day. In 1 Samuel 17:25 the soldiers of Israel were saying, "Have you seen this man who has come up? Surely he has come up to defy Israel."

In other words, Goliath wasn't content to stay on the Philistine side of the street. He was coming right up into the Israeli camp, saying, "Come on! Who's going to fight me? Let's do it! Pick your guy and let's get after it."

He was really bringing the battle right into their faces. That's a reminder that if you tolerate a giant in your life, it will soon take over your territory. It won't stay a mile away or a block away. It will end up on your doorstep, pounding on your front door.

That's why it's never a good strategy to run from giants. You need to attack them.

Don't reason with them, negotiate with them, or offer terms to them. Don't even yell at them. You need to kill them, because that's what David did. Open your Bible to 1 Samuel 17 and underline and highlight verse 48, because it's classic.

It says: "As Goliath moved closer to attack, David quickly *ran* out to meet him" (NLT, emphasis mine).

David didn't just hold his ground or look for a defensible position; he *ran* toward the giant. How does this apply to you and me? Let's get practical. Maybe your problem is lust and you've been feeding it with pornography. Lately it's become a rampaging giant in your life, and you want to be rid of it. You're wondering, *How do I slay the giant?*

First of all, you need to admit that it's sin. It isn't just a problem or an unhealthy habit, it is sin against God. Admit it!

159

Bring it out into the light of day. Make yourself accountable to someone who will pray for you and check in on you. What if it's drinking or drugs that has you bound? Call it what it is and cry out to God for help. Then go on the attack. Instead of trying to hide, get help. Get into a recovery program at a church where people will support you and pray for you. Instead of hesitating or worrying or hiding in the shadows, bring your problem into the light of day and run toward the battle line.

Finish Your Giant Off

Don't just attack your giants. Kill them. Finish them off. Here is what David did.

> Reaching into his shepherd's bag and taking out a stone, he hurled it with his sling and hit the Philistine in the forehead. The stone sank in, and Goliath stumbled and fell face down on the ground. (1 Sam. 17:49 NLT)

It is interesting that the stone hit Goliath right in the forehead. It wasn't a random, lucky shot. David was quite adept with a sling. He'd had lots and lots of time to practice while he was out with the sheep all day.

Jonathan got his boy, Christopher, my grandson, a slingshot for Christmas. (Nothing says Christmas like a slingshot, right?) It's one of those old-school slingshots with a Y-shaped piece of wood and a big rubber band. Christopher has been shooting stuff like crazy, but thankfully he hasn't had the opportunity to practice with large predators.

Goliath had a massive sword, spear, and javelin, and David had an early-model slingshot. What's today's equivalent? Goliath had an assault rifle and David had a squirt gun.

But David was not only a skilled marksman, he also benefited from a guided missile. That rock was guided by the hand of God, hitting the giant in one of the few places not covered by armor. The stone was slung with such great velocity that it didn't just bounce off Goliath's thick head, it sank in! Was he dead? Maybe or maybe not. He was lying there and who would have stopped him from getting back up again?

David did. He ran over to the sprawled warrior to finish him off.

How many times in movies and TV shows have we seen a bad guy fall to the ground only to get back up and attack the good guy unawares? The hero is on his phone or turns his back for some reason, and then the villain rises silently and prepares to attack. We're all screaming, "Look behind you! Look behind you!" That kind of mistake wasn't going to happen here. David had seen those movies and never turned his back on this hombre for a minute.

The Bible tells us that David pulled Goliath's supersized sword from its sheath (it probably took both arms) and used it to cut off the giant's head.

It may have even taken a bit of time.

David finished Goliath off and put him to death, and that is how you and I must deal with giants. If we don't kill our giants, they will come back to kill us.

When I was a little boy I used to catch and collect snakes. I have no idea why, but that's what I did and I loved doing it. The way you catch a snake is to step on its body and then reach down and grab it by the neck. You have to hold it very tight, because it will bite you. And then you grab the rest of the snake with your other hand and put it in a bag. (I used a pillowcase.)

If you encounter a rattlesnake, I strongly encourage you to back off and let it be, because they are very deadly. But if you were in a situation with a rattler where you had to kill it, here's what you need to know. Don't cut off his rattle, because that will just tick him off. You have to cut off his head with a shovel or whatever you have. And even then, that severed head can bite! I've seen it happen.

That's what David did. There would be no *Goliath 2* movie or sequel to his story. David dispatched him from the planet.

How does this apply to our battles? If you want to defeat your giant, you can't do it in stages. You have to make a clean break—and that means burning your bridges.

If you have a problem with alcohol, pour it down the drain and don't go near it again. If you have a problem with drugs, get rid of them. If your struggle is with pornography, put a filter on your computer. And if you can't control yourself around the internet, *disconnect* from the internet. "But Greg," someone will say, "this is the twenty-first century. I can't live without the internet." Yes, you can. People have done it for thousands of years, and you can too. Remember the words of Jesus?

> If your right eye causes you to stumble, gouge it out and throw it away. It is better for you to lose one part of your body than for your whole body to be thrown into hell. And if your right hand causes you to stumble, cut it off and throw it away. It is better for you to lose one part of your body than for your whole body to go into hell. (Matt. 5:29–30 NIV)

Did Jesus actually say that? Yes, He did. And He wasn't talking about literally taking either action. His words were figurative. In that culture, the right eye was perceived as the dominant and best eye, and the right arm as the dominant and best arm.

Jesus was saying, "Whatever you need to do, whatever measures you need to take to get sin out of your life, do it. Take them. If you have a problem with drinking and the friends you normally spend time with drink all the time, here's a news flash. You need new friends."

If you have a history with drugs and want to be free from them, don't hang around people who are doing drugs.

As I mentioned earlier in the book, I came to Christ at the age of seventeen. At the time, I was hanging around with a bunch of druggie kids. At first I tried to reason with them and witness to them, but I wasn't successful in that. I finally realized, "These people can't be my friends anymore." It wasn't long at all before I found a new group of Christian friends and started spending time with them instead. I needed their influence. I needed to watch them and listen to them and draw encouragement from them. Then, as I grew stronger in my faith, I was able to help and encourage them in return.

It seemed pretty drastic at the time, and maybe it was. But I had to walk away from my old friends, my old habits, and my old haunts. If I hadn't, I might have slipped right back into my old lifestyle. In David's terms, I had to attack the giant and finish it off for my own survival.

Others Will Benefit from Your Victory

Something very interesting happened after David prevailed over his giant. Here's how Scripture describes the scene:

When the Philistines saw that their champion was dead, they turned and ran. Then the men of Israel and Judah gave a great shout of triumph and rushed after the Philistines, chasing them as far as Gath and the gates of Ekron. The bodies of the dead and wounded Philistines were strewn all along the road from Shaaraim, as far as Gath and Ekron. Then the Israelite army returned and plundered the deserted Philistine camp. (1 Sam. 17:51–53 NLT)

I don't know about you, but this strikes me as one of the most powerful parts of the whole story. Just moments before, the Israelites had been cowering in fear of their enemy because of Goliath and his taunts. But when David took the giant down, the Israelite army was instantly emboldened. Jumping out of their hiding places, they went on the attack, whooping and hollering and charging the enemy without fear.

They shared in the victory of David. David was the representative of Israel, and when he prevailed, *they* prevailed. They not only chased the Philistines out of their territory but they went back and plundered all their weapons and supplies.

Let me apply this in two ways.

When the Lord in His kindness and strength gives you a victory over something that has been plaguing you for a long time, others will benefit from that conquest. Life isn't just about you! People who know you and love you, people who are close to you, people who work with you, will see what God has done in your life and it will fire up their faith too. The Bible says that Israel gave a great shout of triumph. The Hebrew word for *shout* often includes the meaning of "making a joyful noise" or "shouting for joy."[2] And there is joy for all of us when one of us defeats a giant in the name of Jesus.

Maybe your victory will help your husband or wife or kids as they face secret giants and struggles of their own. Maybe people at work or school or in your carpool will gain fresh courage when they see the supernatural work of God in your life.

But there is an even greater and deeper application here. You and I share in the victory of the greater giant slayer, Jesus Christ. He left Heaven and came to earth to be born in a manger. He voluntarily went to the cross, spilling His blood and taking the sins of the whole world upon Himself. Right before He died, He used one word to summarize what had happened. With His last breath, He cried out the word *tetelestai*. It is accomplished! It is completed! It is finished![3]

What did He mean? Jesus meant that at Calvary, on the cross, He defeated the devil and his demons. The book of Colossians has some of the most encouraging words you will read anywhere. "God made you alive with Christ, for he forgave all our sins. He canceled the record of the charges against us and took it away by nailing it to the cross. In this way, he disarmed the spiritual rulers and authorities. He shamed them publicly by his victory over them on the cross" (2:13–15 NLT).

Jesus defeated the devil. I can't do that and neither can you. We're no match for Satan. He's not the equal of God but he is a powerful spiritual being that you don't want to face in your own strength. But if you belong to Jesus Christ, you have a share in *His* victory, just as the Israelite army shared in David's victory. You have an ID tag attached to you that says, "Property of Jesus Christ."

If you feel defeated or intimidated by a giant, remember that you are in the One who is victorious, and He is in you. He will face down your giant and let you come along for the ride.

8

The Excuses of a World Changer

But Moses said, "Lord, please! Send someone else."

~Exodus 4:13 TLB

When people from older generations hear the name Moses, many of them have a mental image of actor Charlton Heston, who portrayed the great leader of God's people in the epic 1956 movie *The Ten Commandments*. For many, Heston virtually became Moses. In later years, the iconic actor described what the role meant to him. In a 2013 article for *Guideposts* magazine, Heston wrote about the moments in the filming when he "met Moses": "I had met Moses on Sinai, yes, but Moses had met God. And then I knew what Moses had felt, he had been confident, joyous, unhesitating.

"Of course Moses could not lead these thousands across the desert. He never would have tried. But God could do it. And Moses, this all-too-human man, this man so much like the rest of us, had simply turned himself into the instrument through which the strength of God moved."[1]

A younger generation might visualize actor Christian Bale, who played Moses in the more recent film called *Exodus: Gods and Kings*. Bale, however, didn't have the reverence for the biblical account that Heston did. In my opinion, he never really understood who Moses was.

In an interview just before the release of *Exodus*, Bale said this of Moses: "I think the man was likely schizophrenic and was one of the most barbaric individuals that I ever read about in my life."[2] He also described Moses as a "terrorist to the Egyptian Empire."[3] Picturing this biblical hero as a dark, unhappy person lurking in the shadows, Bale might have been confusing Moses with Batman, one of his earlier roles.

Perhaps a little defensively, Bale also said this of his Moses role: "You can't out–Heston Charlton Heston."[4] And by the same token, Hollywood can never out-Moses the real, biblical Moses.

Moses wasn't perfect, but the Bible uses five remarkable words to describe him in Deuteronomy 33:1: "Moses the man of God."

What better description could be said of any of us? What else could you desire as an epithet? "That is a true man of God." Or "She is a real woman of God."

I would rather have that said of me a thousand times more than, "He was the richest man in the world," or, "He was the most famous man in the world." Nothing in all of life compares to being a man or woman of God—unless it is hearing Jesus Christ speak the words, "Well done, good and faithful servant," when we arrive at Heaven's front door.

Moses was a flawed man and a failing man, just like all his fellow heroes in the Hebrews 11 Hall of Faith. But he was also a man of God, who took full advantage of the second chance in life that God had given him. Here is how Hebrews 11 sums up his life.

> By faith Moses, when he was born, was hidden three months by his parents, because they saw he was a beautiful child; and they were not afraid of the king's command.
>
> By faith Moses, when he became of age, refused to be called the son of Pharaoh's daughter, choosing rather to suffer affliction with the people of God than to enjoy the passing pleasures of sin, esteeming the reproach of Christ greater riches than the treasures in Egypt; for he looked to the reward. (vv. 23–26)

The passage really begins with the faith of Moses's parents, a godly Hebrew couple named Amram and Jochebed. Without their courage and faith, there would be no story here at all. They weren't afraid of the king, an all-powerful ruler who had the authority to snuff out their lives on a whim. No, it would seem that they feared and revered the God of Israel more than an earthly Pharaoh.

Most of us have heard the story of how they protected their infant at a time when Pharaoh was seeking to put all the Jewish baby boys to death. Amram and Jochebed hid the baby for as long as they could, then tucked him into a little waterproof basket and placed him in the reeds alongside the Nile—in the hands of a faithful God.

Found in the water and adopted by none other than Pharaoh's daughter, Moses grew up as a prince and prospered in the court of Pharaoh. As Stephen tells us in the book of Acts, "Moses was educated in all the wisdom of the Egyptians and was powerful in speech and action" (7:22 NIV). Some have speculated that Moses may have been a potential successor to Pharaoh, one of the most powerful men in the world at that time.

That's where we pick up the story in Hebrews 11. It was by faith, the Bible tells us, that Moses refused to be treated as the son of Pharaoh's daughter. Instead, "He chose to share the oppression of God's people instead of enjoying the fleeting pleasures of sin. He thought it was better to suffer for the sake of Christ than to own the treasures of Egypt, for he was looking ahead to his great reward (vv. 25–26 NLT).

It's an interesting statement, isn't it? Moses thought it was better to suffer for the sake of the Messiah, who had not yet come, than to own the treasures of Egypt—which could have been his for the taking! For Moses in those days, the world was his oyster. He could have had anything he wanted. He had affluence and influence. The most beautiful clothing. The best meals. The finest education. Probably any Egyptian woman he might have desired. And if he played his cards right, he might have become the most important man on the face of the earth.

But underneath those rich, princely garments beat the heart of a Jew. His fellow Hebrews were suffering terrible oppression under the cruel taskmasters of Egypt. And there came a point in his life where he had to decide what he would do. If he cared about what happened to his people, he could no longer keep his title and stay where he was. He had to leave the palace.

Hebrews 11:24 says, "he grew up" and then made a decision about his destiny. I heard that statement a lot in my younger days. Teachers and coaches and principals would say to me: "Greg Laurie, will you just grow up?" They said that because I was a prankster and always clowning around and getting into trouble, I wasn't growing up as quickly as people wanted me to or thought I should.

Now this, of course, is talking about Moses getting older. But it's also about maturing. We need to grow up spiritually. One of the indications of spiritual growth is when we start thinking about others more than ourselves. If Moses had just thought of himself, he would have been like Leonardo DiCaprio on the bow of the *Titanic*, yelling, "I'm king of the world!" And he really would have been.

But Moses wasn't that kind of man. Others were suffering and he was determined to do something to help them. He had the best of motives, but at that time in his life, he wasn't willing to wait for God's timing or God's way.

Right Idea, Wrong Timing

What motivated Moses? He had a heavenly perspective. Hebrews 11 tells us that he was looking ahead to the great reward that God would give him. He wasn't even sure what that was or how it could happen, but in his heart and soul, he knew better things were to come. Perhaps even beyond this life. So he kept looking ahead.

By faith, Moses saw Jesus the Messiah, somewhere out on the horizon of future years. "He thought that it was better to suffer for the promised Christ than to own all the treasures of Egypt" (Heb. 11:26 TLB). He was like Job, who looked up to Heaven in the midst of his suffering and declared, "I know that my redeemer lives, and that in the end he will stand on the earth. And after my skin has been destroyed, yet in my flesh I will see God; I myself will see him with my own eyes—I, and not another. How my heart yearns within me!" (19:25–27 NIV).

But Moses went and made a big mess of things. He had the right idea, but he certainly went about it the wrong way. You know the story. He saw an Egyptian slave driver mistreating a Jew. So Moses looked to the right, looked to the left, and then killed the Egyptian official and hid his body in the sand.

A word to the wise here. That's never a good place to hide a body. As soon as the wind blows, everyone will know what happened.

When Pharaoh found out, he realized that Moses would never fit in with the royal family and decided to have him executed to eliminate a potential threat.

So Moses headed for the hills—the hills of Midian, to be precise. And with every step away from Egypt he must have relived his catastrophic failure. *Why did I do it? Why didn't I wait for God's timing? Now it's all over. I've blown my chances forever. I will live in obscurity and pay for my foolishness for the rest of my life.*

Out in the Midian wilderness, he found a family that took him in, and he ended up marrying one of the daughters. He became a shepherd—a lowly, dead-end job in the opinion of any respectable Egyptian. Talk about life change! Moses went from being a prince in the palace to a common sheepherder.

Recommissioned out of a Bush

It must have seemed like premature retirement for a strong, capable, highly educated forty-year-old, but Moses saw no other options. He probably gave up on any idea of God using him—ever. He might have been thinking, *Well, that's it for me.*

Is it any wonder that, forty years later, he was taken completely by surprise when he encountered a flaming bush that wouldn't burn? In spite of giving up on himself, Moses was about to come face-to-face with the God of second chances.

One day Moses was tending the flock of his father-in-law, Jethro, the priest of Midian. He led the flock far into the wilderness and came to Sinai, the mountain of God. There the angel of the LORD appeared to him in a blazing fire from the middle of a bush. Moses stared in amazement. Though the bush was engulfed in flames, it didn't burn up. "This is amazing," Moses said to himself. "Why isn't that bush burning up? I must go see it."

When the LORD saw Moses coming to take a closer look, God called to him from the middle of the bush, "Moses! Moses!"

"Here I am!" Moses replied.

"Do not come any closer," the LORD warned. "Take off your sandals, for you are standing on holy ground. I am the God of your father—the God of Abraham, the God of Isaac, and the God of Jacob." When Moses heard this, he covered his face because he was afraid to look at God. (Exod. 3:1–6 NLT)

God told Moses that He was fully aware of the suffering of the Jewish people in Egypt and that they needed a deliverer to lead them out of slavery and bondage. He was telling Moses, "By the way, that deliverer is *you.*"

Understand that Moses was an octogenarian at this point—a card-carrying senior citizen. He had spent forty years in the court of Pharaoh and forty years leading Jethro's sheep around the wilderness. Presumably he hadn't heard from the Lord for years and didn't imagine he ever would again.

Maybe that's the way you feel right now. You can't even remember the last time you heard from God. Here's something to consider. If you don't feel like the Lord is speaking to you, make sure you have no unconfessed sin in your life. Nothing will cut off communication between you and the Father in Heaven faster than sin that has not been acknowledged and confessed. In Isaiah 59 the Lord says, "Listen! The LORD's arm is not too weak to save you, nor is his ear too deaf to hear you call. It's your sins that have cut you off from God. Because of your sins, he has turned away and will not listen anymore" (vv. 1–2 NLT).

Christ taught us to pray in Luke 11:4, "Forgive us our sins, as we forgive those who have sinned against us" (NLT). And David said, "Search me, O God, and know my heart; test my thoughts. Point out anything you find in me that makes you sad, and lead me along the path of everlasting life" (Ps. 139:23–24 TLB). Confessing our sins, known and unknown, is something we need to do every day of our lives. As we do, we will experience His grace, forgiveness, and full restoration.

In the case of Moses, it wasn't unconfessed sin. It was *timing*. Until the day when he encountered the burning bush, he wasn't quite ready. But at the right moment, the Lord recommissioned him—out of a bush!

It was an unremarkable desert bush. It was an ordinary bush doing an extraordinary thing. God could have sent Gabriel in shining raiment, or one of the mighty angels who so overwhelmed Daniel that the prophet fell at his feet like a dead man (see Dan. 10:9).

But no, God used a simple briar bush, consumed with supernatural flame. Why do you think the Lord chose that bush? In a way, it was like a picture of Moses. He was like an old desert bush that God ignited. Or maybe it's a picture of you. God is about to recommission you at an unlikely time, in an unlikely place, in an unlikely way. God may come to you and say, "I've got a plan for your life. I want to use you for My purposes and for My glory."

Sometimes these divine opportunities might come disguised as interruptions in our schedule. We ask ourselves, "Why did this happen?" "Why did I get a flat tire?" "Why did I end up in the hospital?" "Why am I out of a job?" "Why am I on this lengthy detour?"

Our disappointments can become divine appointments. The interruptions can be divine interventions. That was what was happening to Moses. He was eighty years old, with skin as weathered and tanned as saddle leather. His windblown hair and beard probably even made him look like a desert bush. And the Lord picked that moment to call him into kingdom service.

This is a reminder that God doesn't just call young people. He calls all people at every stage in life.

When we get older, we tend to become more conservative and set in our routines. We tend to wear certain kinds of clothing, watch the same TV shows, eat at the same restaurants, and even sit in the same seats in church. We like to know what's coming.

When we're young, we're more willing to take risks. We're willing to just go for it. But when we get older, we might find ourselves saying, "I don't know if I want to try that. I'll think about it right after my nap."

Moses was well past retirement age. He could have replied to the Lord, "I've worked hard for forty years chasing these sheep around. I've earned some 'me time.' I want to kick back and take it easy for a change."

But God still had a plan for Moses's life. He wasn't finished with him by a long shot. And by the way, He still has a plan for you too. Hebrews 12:1 says, "Let us run with perseverance the race marked out for us" (NIV). If you belong to Jesus Christ, there is a race marked out for you. If you ask Him for guidance, the Lord will make that path clear to you.

Never doubt that. God wants to use all of us at every stage of our lives.

The Lord was telling Moses, "I'm recommissioning you, son. Park the Winnebago, cancel the watercolor classes, and let's get busy. We've got work to do."

Excuses, Excuses, Excuses

What Moses *should* have done in that moment was fall down on his face in the sand and say, "Thank You, Lord, for this second chance! I'm ready to go. Lead on!" But that's not what happened. Instead, with his mind whirling, the former prince of Egypt began to offer up excuse after excuse for why he couldn't serve the Lord. The implication? "Lord, You must be mistaken. You must have meant some other old shepherd standing in front of some other old bush. Obviously, You couldn't mean *me!*"

We do the same thing, don't we? Even though we know deep down that God has a plan for our lives and that He can enable us and empower us to do His will, we can still think of a dozen reasons why it won't work.

See if any of these excuses sound strangely familiar to you.

"I Don't Deserve to Be Used by God"

But Moses protested to God, "Who am I to appear before Pharaoh? Who am I to lead the people of Israel out of Egypt?" (*Exod. 3:11 NLT*)

In a way, Moses had a point. If you were God, would you have picked Moses? Why not pick some young guy? Why pick a murderous felon to be the leader of Your people? Moses had a lot of baggage and hadn't updated his résumé for about forty years. Why use him?

That's one of the interesting things about serving this God of ours. He seems to go out of His way to pick the most unexpected and unlikely people for His purposes. When God wanted to reach the people of Nineveh, He called a narrow-minded racist named Jonah, who actually hated Nineveh and everyone in it. He wanted God to kill the Ninevites or make them suffer. But God said, "You're the perfect guy to preach My grace and mercy to these people."

"I don't want to go."

"Whatever. Pack your bag, we're going."

And what was the result? A great revival broke out in that city, changing their destiny for a generation.

But here's a bit of encouraging news. God doesn't see you for what you are. He sees you for what you can become. He sees potential. It is said that the great master artist Michelangelo was looking at a big slab of marble when he said, "I saw an angel in the stone and carved it to set it free."[5]

Michelangelo could just look at a slab of stone and see what could emerge from it. In the same way, God looks at you and says, "I know what you can be. You don't know it yet, but I know. I know what I can make you into. You'll be a mighty man of God. You'll be a powerful woman of God. I don't care if you are young or old. I don't care if you think you're unqualified and ill-equipped. I will work in you and through you so that you can accomplish My purposes."

"I Don't Have All the Answers"

But Moses protested, "If I go to the people of Israel and tell them, 'The God of your ancestors has sent me to you,' they will ask me, 'What is his name?' Then what should I tell them?"

God replied to Moses, "I AM WHO I AM. Say this to the people of Israel: I AM has sent me to you." (Exod. 3:13–14 NLT)

Moses basically asked, "Who are you?" And God replied, "I AM WHO I AM."

It's another way of saying, "Stop talking about yourself, Moses. Stop thinking about yourself and what you will say. Just tell them *I AM* has sent you. It's not about you; it's about Me."

What's one of the main excuses people use for not engaging nonbelievers with the gospel? "What if they ask me a hard question and I don't know the answer? I don't have all the answers."

So what? Just get out there and share your faith. If you don't have an answer for a specific question, go back and study more and you'll have more answers the next time. But don't let not knowing stop you from telling others about Jesus.

"But Greg, I don't know if I can prove the existence of God."

Your job isn't to prove the existence of God. Your job is to proclaim the Good News of the gospel.

"But what if they don't believe in the Bible? Can I still quote it?"

Are you kidding? God says His Word is alive and powerful and sharper than any two-edged sword. That's true whether they believe it or not. Someone may say, "I don't believe in your Bible. I don't think it's inspired by God." And you can reply, "Really? That's interesting." And you can still go ahead and share it with them, letting the supernatural power of God's Word penetrate their hearts. In the book of Isaiah, God says of His Word: "I send it out, and it always produces fruit. It will accomplish all I want it to, and it will prosper everywhere I send it" (55:11 NLT).

In the mid-1990s, I was just getting started with crusade evangelism. The opportunity opened up for me to preach the gospel in arenas and stadiums, but I felt hesitant and overwhelmed by the size of the task.

During that time of indecision, Cathe and I were visiting with Ruth Graham, Billy Graham's wife, at their home in North Carolina. We were often asked to speak at the Billy Graham Training Center at the Cove, which was very close to their home. On this occasion Billy was at a crusade somewhere, but Ruth was home.

She was such a wonderful lady. Fun loving, quick to laugh, knowledgeable in the Scriptures, and full of wisdom.

One day I opened my heart to her and said, "Ruth, I'm intimidated about doing these crusades. I don't feel like I'm ready for it. I think I need to brush up on my apologetics." Ruth looked at me and said, "Don't worry about that, Greg.

You just proclaim the gospel. That's what Billy always did. That's what you need to do."

"Yes, ma'am."

She was right. And as the years have gone by, my evangelistic messages have grown simpler and more basic. My goal is to make the message understandable, not assuming that my listener has a clue as to what I'm actually talking about, and not assuming that people know biblical terminology, because most people don't nowadays.

If they reject the message, let it be because they are opposed to it or don't like it, not because they don't understand it.

"The People Won't Believe Me"

But Moses protested again, "What if they won't believe me or listen to me? What if they say, 'The LORD never appeared to you'?" (Exod. 4:1 NLT)

The Lord said to Moses, "What do you have there in your hand?"

Moses replied, "What? This? It's a shepherd's staff."

"Throw it to the ground," the Lord said. Moses obeyed and the stick became a snake. Moses was terrified and ran away from it.

This is funny to me. It was probably a cobra, and Moses didn't want any part of it. But then the Lord told him to grab the snake, so Moses grabbed it by the tail and it became a shepherd's staff again. The Lord told him, "Perform this sign and they will believe you. They will realize that the Lord God of their ancestors, the God of Abraham, Isaac, and Jacob has appeared to you."[6]

Now this is crazy because, like I said, you never grab a snake by the tail. It will immediately turn around and bite you. Why did God say to grab the snake? Because the snake, particularly the cobra, was a symbol of Egypt. You can look at the antiquities of that nation today and see the cobra symbolizing Egypt, and Pharaoh in particular.

So God was saying, in essence, "I am more powerful than the snake. I am more powerful than Egypt and its Pharaoh."

In our modern vernacular we speak of grabbing a tiger by the tail. In other words, don't be intimidated. Face your fears and remind yourself that the Lord is greater than all of them. That's what Moses did. He picked up the cobra because he was being commissioned by God. And we have been commissioned by the Lord to represent Christ to a pagan culture as well.

Moses was called to the pagan culture of Egypt. We're called to the pagan culture of the United States of America and to the rest of the world. And when I use the term *pagan* I mean that descriptively, not in a derogatory way. I'm speaking of a people who believe in anything and everything but the right thing.

There was a time in our history, because of our Judeo-Christian foundation, when there was a stronger belief in God and the Bible and higher church attendance. Those days are now behind us. Many people in our country today know almost nothing about Scripture and understand very little about Christ Himself. I don't think most Americans have even heard an accurate presentation of the gospel.

God was recommissioning Moses to reach His people in a pagan culture dominated by false gods and evil spirits, and we have been commissioned as well. The world may not believe our words, but we are still called to share God's message.

"I'm Not a Good Speaker"

But Moses pleaded with the LORD, "O Lord, I'm not very good with words. I never have been, and I'm not now, even though you have spoken to me. I get tongue-tied, and my words get tangled." (Exod. 4:10 NLT)

Moses wasn't impressing the Lord with this argument at all. Not even a little bit. The fact is, God isn't looking for good speakers; He is looking for obedient servants.

You don't have to be a great orator to be an effective communicator for the Lord. You just need to be someone who obeys God. He will give you the right words when you need them, because God is more interested in character than charisma. I'm confident in the power of that message and have witnessed the transformation of the lives of thousands of men and women. That's why I keep proclaiming God's message every chance I get.

You have the same message, and you need to present it in your own way, using the unique set of gifts in the unique circumstances that God has given you.

"I'm Not Qualified"

But Moses said, "Lord, please! Send someone else." (Exod. 4:13 TLB)

In the New King James Version, this verse reads, "O my Lord, please send by the hand of whomever else You may send." That's a fancy way of saying, "Get someone else to do it. There's someone else, send *him!*"

It's almost comical to hear Moses explaining his speech impediments to the Lord. He's saying, "It's embarrassing. I stumble over my words. I have this stuttering thing. Obviously, I'm not Your guy. You need to find someone else. My brother, Aaron, maybe? He used to have the gift of gab."

As if the Lord didn't know all of Moses's limitations already! As if He hadn't already taken all of that into account! But in spite of it all, He was calling Moses and knew perfectly well how to equip him for the task.

I'm reminded of my friend Pastor Jack Hibbs of Calvary Chapel, Chino Hills. Jack walked into a Bible study I was teaching years ago. Why did he show up at this particular event? Because he had been driving around, noticed a carload of cute girls pulling into the church parking lot, and simply followed them in. He was a nonbeliever, but he was curious. Where were those girls going? He thought it must be a party. He walked into the church auditorium, where I was speaking that night. And before the Bible study was over, Jack had accepted Christ.

As the days went by, he had no idea what God wanted to do with his life. The fact is, he had a serious problem with stuttering, and couldn't even speak a single sentence without difficulty. Eventually he married a Christian woman and kept right on praying about God's will for his life. How could God use someone who couldn't even get a sentence out without stammering?

And then he ran headlong into a miracle of God. The very first time he shared the gospel with someone, the stuttering went away and never returned. Now he is a pastor and a very effective communicator.

The Lord can turn a disability into an ability. Hebrews 11 speaks of those "whose weakness was turned to strength" (v. 34 NIV). In Moses's case, he had simply lost his confidence.

As a young man Moses was mighty in words and deeds. And the Lord knew that he could be that again.

So what's the bottom line here? Stop offering lame excuses, because they're not legit. There's no reason why you can't be used by God. Ask Him to open doors for you and take advantage of every opportunity to serve Him that comes your way, leaning on Him for strength and ability.

Ultimately, Moses stopped arguing and set about doing what the Lord called him to do. And in the process, he changed his world.

Was it easy? Of course not. As Moses went out to proclaim his message of deliverance for the Lord's people, Pharaoh was as stubborn and intransigent as a brick wall. It will be the same for us at times. When we decide to do God's will, the devil isn't going to help us. He will oppose us with everything he has. But what he has isn't enough to frustrate God's purposes, as Pharaoh and the armies of Egypt discovered the hard way.

The Lord will work through anyone who stays alert to opportunities and steps forward in faith when He opens the door.

How will He work through you?

Wait and see. That's part of the great adventure.

The World Changer Who Faced Long Odds

Sir, how can *I* save Israel? My family is the poorest
in the whole tribe of Manasseh, and I am the least
thought of in the entire family!

~Judges 6:15 TLB

It's been said that mirrors don't lie. But then again, they don't tell the whole truth, do they?

What do you see when you look in the mirror? If you have one of those lighted, magnifying mirrors, it could almost be a traumatic event. You might prefer a quick glance from a few feet away—preferably with steam on the glass.

What does God see when He looks at you? He sees things differently than you and I do, because we're only looking skin-deep. When Paul wrote to the church at Ephesus, he used these amazing words: *"For we are God's masterpiece. He has created us anew in Christ Jesus, so we can do the good things he planned for us long ago"* (Eph. 2:10 NLT, emphasis mine).

The Greek word translated "masterpiece" in this verse is *poiēma*, from which we get our word "poem."[1] Maybe you don't feel much like a masterpiece or a poem. But that's because you and I don't see the way our Creator sees.

When I look in the mirror, I see flaws and weaknesses, and I notice that the years haven't been overly kind to my face or my profile. When God looks at me, He sees my potential. He not only sees what I was and what I am right now but also what I *could be* through His grace and strength. I see my past; He sees my future. I see a lump of clay; He sees a sculpture. I see random marks on a canvas; God sees a work of art in the making. I see a piece of coal; God sees a sparkling diamond. I see a vacillating, unsure Simon; God sees Peter the rock.

God has a different perspective than we do.

Remember the Lord's words to the prophet Samuel, who thought he spotted Israel's future king in a lineup of David's tall, handsome brothers. "Don't judge by his appearance or height, for I have rejected him. The LORD doesn't see things the way you see them. People judge by outward appearance, but the LORD looks at the heart" (1 Sam. 16:7 NLT).

In this chapter, we'll get a closer look at a man who seemed to have no potential whatsoever. In his own eyes, he certainly didn't. Yet he became a bona fide world changer. His name was Gideon.

The reference to Gideon in the Hebrews 11 Hall of Faith is pretty short. He's lumped in with a number of others in a section that might be called, "If I had time, I'd talk about these guys too."

And what more shall I say? For the time would fail me to tell of Gideon and Barak and Samson and Jephthah, also of David and Samuel and the prophets. (v. 32)

In some ways, it's a little surprising he made it into this roll call of great names at all. Gideon's story doesn't have the best beginning and, quite frankly, it doesn't have an inspiring conclusion either. But God didn't put the list of heroes in Hebrews 11 up for a vote. It was He who included Gideon in this exclusive recitation of courageous men and women who put their faith into action.

Gideon did exercise faith when it counted, yes. But for a big chunk of his life, he was probably pretty average. This should provide hope to people who see themselves on the ordinary, rather than the extraordinary, side of the ledger. Maybe, like me, you weren't the best student. You weren't class president or voted most likely to succeed, and no one ever accused you of being the most handsome or beautiful. When it came time to pick softball teams in PE, you were one of the last ones chosen.

(Unfortunately, that was me. At the end, it would be between me and a three-legged dog—and I would still come in last.)

Here's something that may be hard for average Janes and Joes like us to process: God goes out of His way to find and use people like us. He loves to tap ordinary people on the shoulder and ask them to accomplish extraordinary things for His kingdom. Why? So the glory for what's accomplished goes to Him—which happens to be the best possible outcome in the universe. The regular, nonflashy individuals who find themselves on the action end of a miracle are more likely to say, "Praise God! I could have never done that on my own."

These are the people God uses. These are the people who change their world.

His World in a Mess

Gideon's world needed changing—big time.

The people of his era were morally upside down, because they were spiritually upside down. Wherever there is a spiritual breakdown, there will be a moral breakdown, followed by a cultural breakdown.

The verse that pretty much explains everything is Judges 17:6: "In those days there was no king in Israel; everyone did what was right in his own eyes."

Let me paraphrase that: Everybody just did their own thing.

It reminds me of the culture we live in today. Have you heard people talk about "your truth" and "my truth"? Someone will say, "That's *your* truth. I don't believe in *your* truth. I have *my own* truth. I will do what I want to do and live by the dictates of my own conscience." They might even throw God into the mix, and say, "God just wants me to be happy."

In essence, they're just making up their own god and their own morality as they go along. They do whatever they can get away with or feel like doing.

So God raised up judges in those days to rule over Israel and to bring some order to the turmoil. There were thirteen judges in all, twelve men and one woman over a period of about three hundred and fifty years. I don't think these were like district or Supreme Court judges, running around in black robes with gavels in their hands. These were more like lawmen of the old West. Think of Wyatt Earp showing up in Tombstone, Arizona, trying to bring some law and order. Many of these judges were salty characters and fierce warriors to boot.

Two hundred years had passed since Israel had marched out of Egypt. In the days of Joshua, the nation had chalked up fabulous military victories and conquered much of the land of Canaan. But even though they had seen towering walls fall into the dust and mighty armies melt away before them by the power of God, the Israelites never finished the job. And it was a job that really, really needed finishing.

God told Israel to drive out the inhabitants of Canaan, the Canaanites, which included the Amorites, the Hittites, the Ammonites, the Jebusites, the parasites, and all the other "ites." But the victory march stalled, and rather than obeying God, the Israelites shrugged their shoulders and let the remaining Canaanites stick around.

It was a catastrophic mistake. Not only would the Canaanites come back to haunt God's people but in some cases, they would rule over and cruelly oppress them.

This same dynamic can happen to Christians sometimes. We commit our lives to the Lord and say, "Lord, You can have the keys to every door of my life—except for maybe those two doors over there. You can have everything, Lord, but please leave my finances alone—or my marriage, or my career, or my habits that I don't want to give up." But if I don't want Him to be Lord of all, is He really Lord at all?

Israel allowed pockets of Canaanites in the land by not driving them out, and those pockets continued to grow and get stronger. And then they came back with a vengeance.

Where did this apathy and foolishness come from? It really began when Israel turned from the God of their fathers and began to worship corrupt, demonic idols.

That set the stage for what happened next.

> Then the people of Israel began once again to worship other gods, and once again the Lord let their enemies harass them. This time it was by the people of Midian, for seven years. The Midianites were so cruel that the Israelis took to the mountains, living in caves and dens. (Judg. 6:1–2 TLB)

Imagine, then, that you are an Israelite and one day you look up at the southeast horizon and see a vast host of Midianites, armed to the teeth and riding camels. And this was no courtesy call. The wild invaders from the desert were there to raid, rape, steal, trample, and kill.

> These enemy hordes arrived on droves of camels too numerous to count and stayed until the land was completely stripped and devastated. So Israel was reduced to abject poverty because of the Midianites. Then at last the people of Israel began to cry out to the Lord for help. (Judg. 6:5–7 TLB)

In their fearful and desperate situation, the Israelites suddenly remembered their God and began to cry out to Him for help. We might say, "Well, if they had called on Him earlier, they wouldn't have found themselves in such a mess." True. But when the pinch came, they really did turn to Him again.

There's nothing wrong with calling out to the Lord in a moment of crisis. Let me take that one step further. You are stupid if you *don't* call on God in a moment of crisis.

I've heard people say, "Christianity is just a crutch for weak people."

When I hear something like that, I reply, "Christianity isn't a crutch. Christianity is a whole hospital!" I'm not ashamed to admit I lean on God every day of my life. And it's strange how it works out. The harder I lean, the better I do in life.

If you have half a brain, call on Him. Cry out to Him. Block out everything else and pour out your heart to the almighty God. He will hear you on a sunny, blue-sky day, and He will hear you in the middle of a storm so stressful you can hardly put two thoughts together. In Jeremiah 33:3, God said, "Call to Me, and I will answer you, and show you great and mighty things, which you do not know." Some of the things "you do not know" may very well include the answers to your most perplexing problems and deepest needs.

The Lord heard Israel's prayer, too, and He was about to answer it in a highly unusual way. He was about to call on an insignificant farmhand named Gideon.

The Reluctant Warrior

As our story begins, we find Gideon trying to prepare a little bit of wheat while crouching behind the walls of a small winepress. It was hardly a picture of heroism and courage. Like the rest of Israel, he was hungry, hurting, and humiliated. And the Lord said, "I've found My man."

> Then the angel of the LORD came and sat beneath the great tree at Ophrah, which belonged to Joash of the clan of Abiezer. Gideon son of Joash was threshing wheat at the bottom of a winepress to hide the grain from the Midianites. The

angel of the LORD appeared to him and said, "Mighty hero, the LORD is with you!"

"Sir," Gideon replied, "if the LORD is with us, why has all this happened to us? And where are all the miracles our ancestors told us about? Didn't they say, 'The LORD brought us up out of Egypt'? But now the LORD has abandoned us and handed us over to the Midianites."

Then the LORD turned to him and said, "Go with the strength you have, and rescue Israel from the Midianites. I am sending you!" (Judg. 6:11–14 NLT)

I love how the Lord greets Gideon in verse 12: "Mighty hero, the LORD is with you!"

What kind of compliment is that to say to a guy who's hiding? That would be like approaching some poor kid who can't throw a football right and saying, "Hey, Tom Brady, how's it going?" Or maybe walking up to a little girl who's failing math class and saying, "How are you doing, Einstein?"

It almost sounds like mockery. Gideon didn't feel like a mighty hero; he felt like a pathetic zero. Nevertheless, this was the angel of the Lord talking, and He was dead serious. But as I have noted, God not only sees who we are, He sees who we could become.

Gideon's response was interesting. He started complaining! Did he really know who he was talking to? He was saying, "Why has all this happened to us?" and "Where are all the miracles we heard about in the old days?"

God could have rebuked Gideon. He could have said, "Are you kidding Me? You guys brought this on yourselves. It's just what I said would happen if you turned from Me and started chasing after foreign gods." But the Lord didn't do that. He effectively said, "We've got a job to do, Gideon. Let's get going."

It's like trying to get the kids ready to go somewhere and loading them into the car. You're searching for a doll. One of the kids is missing a shoe. Someone else is whining that they're hungry. Pretty soon, Mom or Dad has to say, "*Just get in the car. We'll sort it all out later. Let's go!*"

It's as though the Lord was saying, "Gideon, I don't have time to deal with your whining and your lame questions. This is going down, and we're starting right now." But once again, Gideon protested. "'But Lord,' Gideon replied, 'how can I rescue Israel? My clan is the weakest in the whole tribe of Manasseh, and I am the least in my entire family!'" (Judg. 6:15 NLT).

A modern interpretation of that last statement might be: "I'm the runt of the litter. I'm the lowest of the low." But God replied, "And you're just the guy I want."

Let's consider a few principles about world changers that we can take away from Gideon's story.

World Changers Are Humble

Gideon was genuinely humble. If people have to tell you how humble they are, they're only looking for attention and affirmation. But Gideon had no illusions about who he was. In verse 15, Gideon seems to be saying, "Who am I that You would call me?"

I love the Lord's response: "I will be with you. And you will destroy the Midianites as if you were fighting against one man" (v. 16 NLT). In other words, "It's not about who you are, Gideon, it's about who I am. I'm the One who will be with you and enable you to do these things. So let's get going."

The Lord gives him these words of reassurance, but there would still be another important test before Gideon led anyone into battle. And the test would be in his own home.

World Changers Are Faithful in the Little Things

In Judges 6:25–26, God told Gideon to tear down the altar his father, Joash, had erected to one false god and cut down the pole dedicated to another one. Then he was to build an altar to the true God on the hilltop, cut up the pole for firewood, and sacrifice his dad's prize bull on the altar.

And he did it. Gideon did everything the Lord told him to do. But it wasn't easy.

> So Gideon took ten of his servants and did as the LORD had commanded. But he did it at night because he was afraid of the other members of his father's household and the people of the town. (Judg. 6:27 NLT)

If you want God to use you to do big things, you first have to start with little things.

Tearing down a false idol and sacrificing his dad's cow wasn't like taking on a huge Midianite army, but it was a frightening first step for Gideon.

In the early seventies, as a brand-new Christian, I started attending Calvary Chapel of Costa Mesa. I made an appointment to see Pastor Chuck Smith. This was a small step that seemed like a big leap to me. The pastor invited me into his office, and I sat down in front of his large desk.

"Pastor Chuck," I began, "I want to be used by God. I want to serve the Lord here."

In the back of my mind I was thinking he might ask me to teach one of the Bible studies at the church—maybe work my way up to preaching for him on a Sunday morning.

Pastor Chuck said, "Okay, Greg. That's good. I'm glad you want to serve the Lord. I want you to go talk to one of my associate pastors. His name is Pastor Romaine."

I didn't have any idea who Pastor Romaine was, but I found out fast enough. He was a former drill sergeant in the Marine Corps. I came walking up to him, a young hippie kid in sandals with shoulder-length hair, and said, "Hi, I'm here to serve the Lord and Chuck sent me to you."

Apparently Pastor Romaine knew exactly what that meant. Free janitorial work!

"Well, that's fine, Greg," he said. "Here's a broom. I'd like you to sweep the hallways. And when you're done, the restrooms could use some attention."

I must have just stared at him for a few seconds. I remember thinking, *Excuse me. I didn't volunteer to be a janitor and clean toilets. I volunteered to serve the Lord.*

But these pastors understood that if I couldn't be faithful in the little tasks, they wouldn't be able to trust me with anything greater. As a result, they got a lot of free labor out of me. Over time, however, my responsibilities began to increase. Some days I would answer the phone. A few times I was asked to counsel someone. Then came the day when I made a hospital call. Not long after that, I found myself teaching a little Bible study.

In Luke 16:10, the Lord said, "If you are faithful in little things, you will be faithful in large ones" (NLT).

God gave Gideon a small task that still required a huge step of faith. And Gideon did it.

Some might be critical of the way he did it, saying, "Hey, he waited until the middle of the night and did it in secret. If he really trusted God, he would have done it in broad daylight." And I say, so what? He heard the Lord and obeyed Him. There will always be people ready to criticize you when you step out to serve the Lord. These are the people who think God gave them the gift of criticism. They're always quick to point out what you are doing wrong. They never have answers, and don't really want to be part of the solution. They would rather throw rocks from the outside.

I've been told, "Greg, we don't like the way you do your evangelism. We don't like the crusade format. We don't like the way you call people to Christ. You don't do it right."

I might reply (or be tempted to reply), "Okay, how do *you* do it?"

"We don't. That's not our calling."

"To tell you the truth, I like my way of doing it better than your way of not doing it."

Of course, our methods aren't perfect. And as the book of James assures us, we all stumble in many ways (see 3:2). But our team is doing the best we can to reach people with the gospel in today's world.

Maybe Gideon should have announced with trumpets, "Let it be known to the whole village that I'm about to pull down the idol of Baal that you have been worshiping, and then I intend to build an altar to the true and living God on top of the hill—where I will proceed to offer a sacrifice to the Lord!"

But he didn't do that. He slipped out at night with the hired help and got the job done, just as the Lord had asked. It's easy to be an armchair quarterback. But world changers are willing to put it all on the line. They're willing to take chances and take risks.

Gideon didn't have long to wait for a response.

> Early the next morning, as the people of the town began to stir, someone discovered that the altar of Baal had been broken down and that the Asherah pole beside it had been cut down. In their place a new altar had been built, and on it were the remains of the bull that had been sacrificed. The people said to each other, "Who did this?" And after asking around and making a careful search, they learned that it was Gideon, the son of Joash.
>
> "Bring out your son," the men of the town demanded of Joash. "He must die for destroying the altar of Baal and for cutting down the Asherah pole." (Judg. 6:28–30 NLT)

But then came an interesting and rather amazing twist in the story. Guess who stepped up to defend Gideon?

> But Joash shouted to the mob that confronted him, "Why are you defending Baal? Will you argue his case? Whoever pleads his case will be put to death by morning! If Baal truly is a god, let him defend himself and destroy the one who broke down his altar!" From then on Gideon was called Jerub-baal, which means "Let Baal defend himself," because he broke down Baal's altar. (Judg. 6:31–32 NLT)

Gideon's dad stepped in front of that angry rabble, telling them, "Let Baal defend himself." I think deep down inside

Joash was proud of Gideon. Maybe the family had been going along with the town's idolatry to be politically correct or because they didn't want to make waves. But it may have been that Gideon's brave act stirred up and rekindled Joash's faith. Whatever the case, the mob backed off.

World Changers Share Their Faith

This brings up an important point. The first place you need to take a stand for your faith in Christ is with the members of your family—with your father, mother, husband, wife, son, daughter, and your extended family. It doesn't have to be elaborate. Just tell them, "I am now a follower of Jesus Christ. I have placed my faith and trust in Him."

They may be skeptical. After all, they've known you since you were in diapers. They might think to themselves, *What's this kid going to tell me next?* Or maybe, *This is just a phase. They'll get over it.*

The answer to this kind of skepticism is for you to simply live life, letting the Lord shine through your positive, happy spirit. Stay hopeful and steady when you're going through trials. Return insults with kindness. That will be more powerful than any sermon to those who are watching your life through a critical lens.

Even Jesus didn't reach His friends and family right away. Just to be fair to His siblings, imagine having Jesus for a brother. I can see Mary getting the other kids in the family together and saying, "What's going on here? Can't you just do your chores? Why can't you be like your big brother Jesus? No one ever has to tell Him twice! He just pitches in and does the work cheerfully. Look how obedient He is.

Look how respectful He is to me and your dad. Look how He makes His bed every day. You kids need to be more like Him."

And maybe out in his carpentry shop Joseph made them all little wooden bracelets that spelled out WWJD.

Two of His brothers (really half-brothers), James and Jude, didn't seem to come around until after the resurrection (see John 7:5). The point here is to make your stand at home, but don't expect your family to respond with enthusiasm right away. They will want to see, over the long haul, if you will really live out what you've been talking about.

Gideon passed the first test with flying colors.

Now it was time to gather an army.

The Amazing Shrinking Army

Right off the bat, Gideon rallied 32,000 men to the cause. Not a bad number, actually. But considering that the Midianites had over 100,000 desert troops, armed to the teeth and riding camels, Gideon's number didn't look so great.

The Lord Himself addressed the size of Gideon's army in a totally unexpected way.

So Jerub-baal (that is, Gideon) and his army got up early and went as far as the spring of Harod. The armies of Midian were camped north of them in the valley near the hill of Moreh. The LORD said to Gideon, "You have too many warriors with you. If I let all of you fight the Midianites, the Israelites will boast to me that they saved themselves by their own strength. Therefore, tell the people, 'Whoever is timid or afraid may leave this mountain and go home.'" So 22,000 of them went home, leaving only 10,000 who were willing to fight. (Judg. 7:1–3 NLT)

The Hebrew term here for "go home" is *momentus returnus.* It translates to, "return to mommy." (Not really. I just made that up.) So Gideon assembled an army of 32,000 Hebrews and, when given the chance, 22,000 of them ran home with their tails between their legs. It wasn't exactly a momentous start.

Well, Gideon may have thought, *we'll have to make this work. Figure out some clever battle tactic. We still have 10,000 guys here who aren't afraid.*

I was telling this Bible story to my grandchildren recently, but for some reason I left out the part about the 10,000 men at the stream. My granddaughter Stella piped up and said, "Papa, you forgot the part about when they drank from the spring."

"You're right, Stella," I said. So, of course, I had to go back and tell that part too.

Just when Gideon was getting used to taking on an army of 100,000 with an army one-tenth that size, God told him he needed to make yet another adjustment.

But the LORD told Gideon, "There are still too many! Bring them down to the spring, and I will test them to determine who will go with you and who will not." When Gideon took his warriors down to the water, the LORD told him, "Divide the men into two groups. In one group put all those who cup water in their hands and lap it up with their tongues like dogs. In the other group put all those who kneel down and drink with their mouths in the stream." Only 300 of the men drank from their hands. All the others got down on their knees and drank with their mouths in the stream.

The LORD told Gideon, "With these 300 men I will rescue you and give you victory over the Midianites. Send all the others home." (Judg. 7:4–7 NLT)

This was a test that would reveal the soldiers' attitude toward the enemy. One group immediately flopped down on their stomachs and drank from the stream with their mouths, paying little or no attention to what was going on around them. The other, much smaller group of soldiers was very careful to note what was happening around them. They drank but stayed aware of their surroundings and kept a lookout for their enemy.

Years ago I was leading a tour group in Israel, and we went to the spring where this event probably happened. I wanted to illustrate how God values being awake, alert, and attentive. I asked for a couple volunteers: one to drink the water directly from the spring and another to cup their hands and sip the water carefully.

As they were enacting my little demonstration, however, I happened to notice a sign posted near the spring. It read: DO NOT DRINK THE WATER.

Oh great, I thought. *What an illustration of being alert! Now someone is going to die because of my sermon illustration.* Fortunately, they were okay.

Nevertheless, Gideon's water test really happened, and it left him with only 300 men—down from 32,000. This was the cream of the crop. They were the Delta Force or Navy SEALs of Israel. The elite of the elite.

Maybe at this point Gideon reasoned that a tiny band of warriors like these would need to be armed with huge swords, sharp spears, and massive shields. But that wasn't part of God's plan either. His little army would go armed with pitchers, torches, and rams' horns! After receiving the Lord's final instructions, General Gideon went to work.

He divided the 300 men into three groups and gave each man a ram's horn and a clay jar with a torch in it.

Then he said to them, "Keep your eyes on me. When I come to the edge of the camp, do just as I do. As soon as I and those with me blow the rams' horns, blow your horns, too, all around the entire camp, and shout, 'For the LORD and for Gideon!'" (Judg. 7:16–18 NLT)

That was it. The military strategy for three hundred soldiers to take on one hundred thousand. Three hundred torches and three hundred rams' horns. It was crazy, it was illogical, and it worked.

When the enemy soldiers saw the torches ringing their camp and heard the clamor of horns and shouts, they thought a massive army had come to overrun and destroy them. Confused, panicked, and discombobulated, they drew swords and started killing each other.

Gideon's army, basically outnumbered 450 to 1, won a crushing victory and delivered the nation. This would be like a Pop Warner team going up against the New England Patriots in the Super Bowl and winning—or a Little League team beating the Chicago Cubs in the World Series.

The odds were terrible—which is just the way God wanted it. The favor of the Lord changes any odds.

We Are in a Battle

We, too, are in a battle. A spiritual battle. And it is a war that can't be fought with normal weaponry. In Ephesians 6:12, Paul reminds us that "our fight is not against any physical enemy: it is against organisations and powers that are spiritual. We are up against the unseen power that controls this dark world, and spiritual agents from the very headquarters of evil" (Phillips).

Don't underestimate our enemy, but don't underestimate our God either. The weapons He places in our hands are effective.

> For though we live in the world, we do not wage war as the world does. The weapons we fight with are not the weapons of the world. On the contrary, they have divine power to demolish strongholds. We demolish arguments and every pretension that sets itself up against the knowledge of God, and we take captive every thought to make it obedient to Christ. (2 Cor. 10:3–5 NIV)

This war we are in—the war for our culture, the war for the eternal souls of every man and woman—will never be won by clever strategies or plans. We won't win by organizing protests, marches, or boycotts, or through skillful manipulation of social media. We are going to win by praying and proclaiming the Word of God.

This is no time to retreat, withdraw, back off, try to blend in, or, like Gideon, crouch in the winepress. You don't become a world changer by hiding or withdrawing or going-along-to-get-along. This is the time to step up our game and go into attack mode with spiritual weapons.

What are those weapons? The best one we have in this culture is praying for people's hearts to change and proclaiming the gospel. This is not the time for idleness. This is the time for infiltration and permeation. We need to do everything we can do to make a difference, while we still have time to make a difference.

Make your stand among people that you know, because Jesus is looking for people He can use. To accomplish the impossible, God will often use the unqualified to do the unexpected.

Listen carefully, He might be calling your name right now.

10

"Of Whom the World Was Not Worthy"

Homeless, friendless, powerless—the world didn't deserve them!—making their way as best they could on the cruel edges of the world.

~Hebrews 11:37–38 MSG

Sometimes it seems like the people in our world can be divided into two camps: ordinary and extraordinary.

We know all about the extraordinary people. We see them on TV and in the movies and on social media. They perform heroic acts, win awards, say quotable things, possess great strength or beauty, show flashes of pure genius, possess over-the-top talent, demonstrate superhuman athletic ability, or figure out how to earn great buckets of money. They're surprising, enviable, and way beyond average in so many ways.

We like to read about them. The media likes to showcase them. And we admire their fame from afar.

And then there are the ordinary people, doing regular everyday tasks. We know about them, too, because we *are* them. People raising families, commuting to work, paying off credit cards, waiting for coffee at the drive-through, walking the dog, and doing yard work.

Because we have been referring to Hebrews 11 as the Hall of Faith, we might be tempted to think that it's a record of extraordinary people drawn from the pages of the Old Testament. The cream of humanity's crop.

Well, yes and no.

God certainly chose to honor them by including their names in one of the greatest chapters of the New Testament. But it wasn't because their names were trending on Twitter or their faces were in the newspapers.

God chose to inscribe them in His eternal Word for one reason. At some point in their lives, probably on an otherwise ordinary day, each of them took a step into the dark and the unknown because they believed in God. In each life, there was a flash of sheer, determined faith in the Lord. And that flash was so bright that we're reading about it right now, thousands and thousands of years later.

These were ordinary people like you and me who did extraordinary things through acts of faith. They faced incredibly adverse circumstances, just as you and I do, but they rose above those circumstances, and with God's enabling, changed their world.

Could we change our world? Is that even still possible?

I love the passage in the book of Acts where a group of anti-Christian activists tried to stop the gospel of Jesus from spreading in their city. They dragged some of the believers in front of the authorities and loudly complained, "These who have turned the world upside down have come here too" (17:6). They didn't mean that as a compliment. It was meant as criticism. They were saying, "These crazy Christians disrupt our comfortable status quo, and we don't like it!" Jesus might have called those believers salty. He once told His disciples, "You are the earth's salt. But if the salt should become tasteless, what can make it salt again? It is completely useless" (Matt. 5:13 Phillips).

In other words, they had an edge to their lives. They stood out. Something about them didn't blend in. They weren't bland or tasteless. They made a difference and stirred things up. I'm reminded of the words attributed to the great British preacher G. Campbell Morgan: "Organized Christianity that fails to make a disturbance is dead."

My concern is that believers aren't making a disturbance anymore. Sometimes, in fact, it seems like the world is changing the church more than the church is changing the world. We need to get back to the job God called us to do, because I believe we can still change this world of ours if we will step up to the plate and start using our faith.

The people in the Hebrews 11 Hall of Faith have two things in common with us. Number one, they were really flawed. And number two, they had faith and *did something with it*. In the process they, as Warren Wiersbe pointed out, collected more scars than medals and more pushback than plaudits.[1] But they made a difference, and that's what God wants for our lives too. He wants us to take what faith we have and apply it to the circumstances in our lives—wherever we are and whatever they may be.

It's interesting that the only place Jesus did not do miracles was in His hometown of Nazareth, because of their unbelief. He wanted to heal them, but He wouldn't heal them because of their lack of faith. Here's the bottom line: God is not limited by your circumstances.

"But Greg, you don't know my situation. It's unbelievably complicated." That may be, but it's no problem for God. There is no circumstance He can't untangle; there is no knot He can't untie. It's our unbelief that's the problem. Sometimes we have to be like the desperate dad in Mark 9:24 who said, "Lord, I believe; help my unbelief!"

You don't have to have superfaith. You just have to *use* the faith you have. Put it out there by saying, "Lord, I'm putting my trust in You"—and then take a step or two.

Faith can make the difference between something happening and not happening because without faith, according to Hebrews 11:6, it's impossible to please God. The verse goes on to say that He rewards those who diligently seek Him.

I heard a story about a mom who was reading Bible stories to her little girl. As you might expect, the storybook focused on accounts full of action and excitement—David and Goliath, Jonah and the great fish, the parting of the Red Sea, and the healing of blind Bartimaeus.

After listening appreciatively for a while, the little girl remarked, "Mommy, God was a lot more exciting back then."

The truth is, He is still exciting. It's still exciting to walk with Him and serve Him. And there is nothing like stepping out in faith—even a baby step—and seeing God work in ways we couldn't have imagined.

What the Bible Says about World Changers

Before we move on from Hebrews 11, let's zero in on what the author said about these world changers as he was wrapping up.

> And what more shall I say? For the time would fail me to tell of Gideon and Barak and Samson and Jephthah, also of David and Samuel and the prophets: who through faith subdued kingdoms, worked righteousness, obtained promises, stopped the mouths of lions, quenched the violence of fire, escaped the edge of the sword, out of weakness were made strong, became valiant in battle, turned to flight the armies of the aliens. Women received their dead raised to life again. (Heb. 11:32–35)

World Changers Are Indestructible until God Is Done with Them

They shut the mouths of lions. (v. 33 NLT)

Whose story comes to mind when we hear this?

Right away we think of Daniel, facing a dark lair full of hungry, unhappy lions—and living to tell the story. Daniel, you might remember, was kidnapped from his home in Jerusalem as a teenager and marched off to Babylon as a captive. Along with his friends Shadrach, Meshach, and Abednego, he was taken into the palace of the king, trained in the ways of the Babylonians, and eventually became one of the king's trusted advisers.

Daniel was wise, so the king came to rely heavily on him, which incurred the anger of other royal counselors. Fiercely jealous over this upstart Hebrew, they wanted him taken out. To facilitate this, the jealous counselors set their investigative reporters out to dig up dirt on him, confident that they would uncover some choice skeletons in Daniel's closet. To their great amazement, however, there wasn't any dirt, and there weren't any skeletons. Try as they might, they couldn't identify even a hint of scandal attached to his life. As it says in Daniel 6:4, "They couldn't find anything to criticize or condemn. He was faithful, always responsible, and completely trustworthy" (NLT).

How inconvenient for them! Going back to the drawing board, they decided that the only way to nail him was through his evident faith in the God of Israel.

Everyone knew one thing about Daniel, and it didn't take a detective to uncover it. They knew that Daniel prayed openly—in plain sight of all—three times a day. With that in mind, the counselors hoodwinked the king into signing a decree that no one could pray to any God except him. The punishment for violations? Becoming fast food for a den of ravenous lions.

The law was made official, and Daniel heard about it. What would he do now? What would *you* do? How would you respond if a law was passed in our nation tomorrow that said you can no longer pray publicly? Would you still say grace over your meal in a restaurant? Would you still pray in your home? Daniel did. Check this out.

When Daniel learned that the law had been signed, he went home and knelt down as usual in his upstairs room, with its windows open toward Jerusalem. He prayed three times a day, just as he had always done, giving thanks to his God. Then the officials went together to Daniel's house and found him praying and asking for God's help. (Dan. 6:10–11 NLT)

We've been talking about acts of faith. But take note of what Daniel did here. It wasn't something big and flashy. He didn't shoot out a Tweet or post a selfie on Instagram. He quietly stuck to his practice of calling on God three times a day. He continued his godly routine and didn't let outside events throw him or deter him. He had prayed in front of an open window before, and he continued to do so—even if all the cameras in the kingdom were aimed at him.

Daniel exercised quiet faith in the face of opposition—but it was also very courageous faith. As it turned out, the king was really upset about Daniel's disobedience. He liked Daniel, but he couldn't overrule his own law, with his signature still wet on the document. So Daniel was escorted to the lions' den and tossed in.

And that was that.

But as we know, that wasn't that.

The Bible says that the king couldn't sleep that night, but I'm guessing Daniel slept like a baby. He probably pillowed his head on the flank of one of those powerful lions. Can't you just hear him? "Come over here, Simba. Your belly looks like a good pillow, and I'm going to prop up my feet on your buddy Leo. Sweet dreams." So Daniel took a catnap with some really big cats.

Meanwhile, the king was stressed, concerned, and freaking out. Skipping his breakfast and coffee, he showed up at the entrance to the lions' den the next morning.

> When he got there, he called out in anguish, "Daniel, servant of the living God! Was your God, whom you serve so faithfully, able to rescue you from the lions?"

Daniel answered, "Long live the king! My God sent his angel to shut the lions' mouths so that they would not hurt me, for I have been found innocent in his sight. And I have not wronged you, Your Majesty."

The king was overjoyed and ordered that Daniel be lifted from the den. Not a scratch was found on him, for he had trusted in his God. (Dan. 6:20–23 NLT)

One of God's holy angels stood between Daniel and the lions, and the big cats didn't want anything to do with *him*. Angels are very involved in the lives of believers. The Bible calls them "ministering spirits sent forth to minister for those who will inherit salvation" (Heb. 1:14). We really don't know much about that ministry—and that is by design. Angels are super undercover; Billy Graham called them "God's secret agents." You and I don't know what they are doing or when they are doing it. With supernatural efficiency, they just set about accomplishing God's work. Sort of like SEAL Team 6 with wings and massive supernatural power.

God sent His angels to deliver Daniel, and He will send His angels to deliver you. You are indestructible until God is done with you. Stop stressing out about how long you will live or whether this or that might happen in the future. Life is a matter of doing what you can for God and exercising your faith in the time He allots to you. And then, when your mission is done, He will send His angels to escort you home (see Luke 16:22).

World Changers Are Never Alone

They quenched the power of fire. (Heb. 11:34 NASB)

This statement alludes to the actions of Daniel's friends Shadrach, Meshach, and Abednego in Daniel 3. King Nebuchadnezzar had erected a colossal, solid gold statue of himself and decreed that when the band struck up a certain tune, everyone had to fall down and worship this monstrosity or be thrown into a furnace of fire.

And everyone did bow, very rapidly, except the three young Hebrew men who loved the Lord and wouldn't bow to any idol, whatever the consequences. With his spies everywhere, the king immediately heard about this act of defiance and had the three Hebrews marched to his throne. Amazingly, he gave them one more chance to comply and save their lives.

But the boys would have none of it. Facing the powerful king, here is how they replied: "King Nebuchadnezzar, we do not need to defend ourselves before you in this matter. If we are thrown into the blazing furnace, the God we serve is able to deliver us from it, and he will deliver us from Your Majesty's hand. But even if he does not, we want you to know, Your Majesty, that we will not serve your gods or worship the image of gold you have set up" (Dan. 3:16–18 NIV).

Nebuchadnezzar was so royally ticked off he gave the command to heat up the furnace seven times hotter than usual. It was so hot that the soldiers who took Shadrach, Meshach, and Abednego to the brink of the flames were overcome and died after tossing in the three offenders.

The king was no doubt thinking, *Well, too bad for them, but let this be a lesson to anyone who defies my great power and authority.* But then, as he peered through the furnace door, he had the shock of a lifetime. In the midst of the flames he saw three figures—and then a fourth!—walking about like it was a Sunday stroll through the park. He said, "Weren't

there three men that we tied up and threw into the fire? . . .
Look! I see four men walking around in the fire, unbound
and unharmed, and the fourth looks like a son of the gods"
(Dan. 3:24, 25 NIV).

Who was that fourth man? The king didn't know. But I
believe it was Jesus Christ walking around with Shadrach,
Meshach, and Abednego in the furnace of fire.

Maybe you're in a fiery trial right now. Maybe you've found
yourself in the hot waters of temptation or you're feeling the
heat of some desperate circumstances closing in on you.

The Lord was with Shadrach, Meshach, and Abednego,
and the Lord is with you. He walks with us through our trials. In the book of Isaiah, God promises:

> When you pass through the waters,
>   I will be with you;
> and when you pass through the rivers,
>   they will not sweep over you.
> When you walk through the fire,
>   you will not be burned;
>   the flames will not set you ablaze. (43:2 NIV)

The three Hebrew teenagers weren't delivered *from* the
flames, but they were delivered *through* the flames. They didn't
escape the fiery trial, but they had a wonderful companion
who walked with them. The Lord doesn't promise to keep us
out of the fire, but He does promise to be with us through it all.

World Changers Sometimes Face Persecution

*Others were tortured, refusing to turn from God in order to be
set free. They placed their hope in a better life after the resur-*

rection. Some were jeered at, and their backs were cut open with whips. Others were chained in prisons. Some died by stoning, some were sawed in half, and others were killed with the sword. Some went about wearing skins of sheep and goats, destitute and oppressed and mistreated. They were too good for this world. (Heb. 11:35–38 NLT)

This passage speaks of a second group of faith heroes who had a different outcome than the group we just discussed. They, too, had faith. They, too, trusted God. But they didn't get past the lions. They didn't walk out of the fires. The Red Sea didn't part for them, they didn't gain what was promised, and their dead were not restored to life.

In fact, this second group of world changers suffered greatly, and many of them died. Were they losers? No, they weren't. They were winners just like the first group. The first group of world changers glorified God through *escaping*, like Daniel, Shadrach, Meshach, and Abednego. The second group of world changers glorified God by *enduring*.

You and I don't get to choose which group we will be in, what will happen in our lives, or what hardships and difficulties will come our way. All that we can determine is how we will respond when those trials cross our paths.

The reference to someone being sawed in half may have been speaking about the prophet Isaiah. According to Jewish tradition, he was sawed in half with a wooden saw. Was that just a barbaric act from the unenlightened and distant past? Not at all. Things just as horrific are happening to our brothers and sisters all over the world. Persecution is alive and well. Christian men, women, and children suffer great cruelty and barbaric treatment in nations like North Korea,

China, Russia, and some Islamic nations. People are still being hounded, tortured, and executed simply for owning the name of Jesus. Many terrorist organizations are known for atrocities that rival any of the brutalities detailed in Scripture.

The Bible clearly tells us that "all who desire to live godly in Christ Jesus will suffer persecution" (2 Tim. 3:12). That's a biblical promise we rarely claim. You won't see that inscribed in calligraphy and framed on someone's living room wall. Who wants to be persecuted?

Persecution can take many forms. It can be physical, like a threat against a life, or actually taking that life. It can be verbal, where people mock you, marginalize you, or insult you because of your faith in Jesus Christ. It can even be financial, when a stand for Christ and God's Word hurts your occupation or business.

None of us know for sure how persecution will come, but we shouldn't be surprised when it does. The Bible said it would.

But what should our response be? Here's how Jesus put it in Matthew 5:10–12: "Happy are those who are persecuted because they are good, for the Kingdom of Heaven is theirs. When you are reviled and persecuted and lied about because you are my followers—wonderful! Be *happy* about it! Be *very glad!* for a *tremendous reward* awaits you up in heaven. And remember, the ancient prophets were persecuted too" (TLB).

Just make sure that if you are persecuted, it is for the right reason. There is no blessing waiting for you if you are persecuted or excluded for being rude, obnoxious, or a royal jerk. Let it be because you're a humble, happy, godly follower of Christ.

Trust and Follow Him without an Explanation

We look at the first part of Hebrews 11 and note how God took care of His people. There was suffering involved, but ultimately, they were delivered. Joseph faced some harsh difficulties, but he eventually got out of prison and was put into a position of great authority. David was preserved by the Lord time after time. And yet now, in the later verses of Hebrews 11, we're reading about people being beheaded, tortured, sawed in half, or driven into the wilderness. We might find ourselves thinking, *This isn't fair.*

Children like to say that, don't they? "It isn't fair!" I have five grandkids and I have discovered this important truth. If I buy one of them a gift, I have to buy all of them a gift. And the gifts have to be identical. With the girls, it's easy. If I buy them necklaces, they're all the same. Same color. Same everything. I don't vary even a little. If I ever happened to get one of them something different, then it would automatically become the "best" necklace, and I'd never hear the end of it. "Why didn't we get one like that. Papa, that isn't fair."

I have a grandson, too, so I have to find something of equal value for him, or I will be accused of favoritism.

We say the same things to God sometimes, even if it's never out loud.

"Lord, why am I single and all my friends are married?"

"Lord, why can't I be attractive as they are?"

"Why can't my husband and I conceive children when it seems so easy for others?"

"Why did our child go prodigal when their child stayed on course?"

"Why do I have this horrible illness when all my friends are healthy?"

"Why did my marriage fall apart when no one else in our family is divorced?"

"Why did my child have to die while others get to keep their children?"

I am speaking now from experience; I understand these questions all too well. My own son Christopher died in an automobile accident in 2008 at the age of thirty-three.

We don't know why certain things happen to us or why tragedies enter our lives. Some have said, "You should never ask God why. That's a lack of faith."

No, it isn't. Ask away. Ask God why. He can handle it. Don't expect an answer by return mail. But there is nothing wrong with asking. David and the psalmists asked God questions repeatedly. Even Jesus cried out from the cross, "My God, My God, why have You forsaken Me?" (Matt. 27:46).

God blessed Cathe and me with two boys; one is in heaven and one is here on earth serving the Lord. We are very proud of Jonathan, who is not only walking strong with Christ but serves as a pastor at our church. We are thrilled by that. But even so, we still wish with all our hearts that Christopher were with us right now.

Sometimes I get the idea that people want me to say, "It all turned out great, and we're happy with it." Actually, I'm not happy with it. And if I could change the situation, I'd do so in a heartbeat. But I don't get to make that decision.

So what am I saying? That I'm disappointed with God? Absolutely not. My faith in the Lord remains and grows stronger with each passing year. I trust Him and I look to Him, even though I don't like everything that has happened to our family. But I know He's in control, and I know that His plans for me are better than my plans for myself. What's more? I know that someday all my questions will be answered.

As a pastor, I often meet parents who have lost children. I don't feel like I have the answers for these folks, but I think at least to some degree I understand a little bit of what they're going through, so I listen to them.

But you know what? I'm not in the explaining business anymore. I was in the explaining business in my twenties when I was starting out in ministry. I was an awesome twenty-year-old pastor. I had long hair, I was skinny, and I could eat whatever I wanted. I also had the answer to every question you ever had. I had a verse for everything, and I would give it to you and tell you why you should trust God.

But I'm out of that business now. These days, I feel that I'm more in the trusting and praying business. I'm trusting that God will answer my questions one day, and I'm praying for strength. That's what I share with other people. None of us get to control our circumstances. What we do get to control, with God's help, is our reaction to those circumstances.

Hebrews 11:35 tells us "women received their dead raised to life again." And we might remember here how Elijah raised the widow's son to life, or Jesus raised up Lazarus, or Paul restored poor Eutychus to life after he fell out of a three-story window.[2]

That's great. But guess what? They all had to die again. (Which seems like a lousy deal, if you ask me.) That's because everybody dies.

It doesn't mean that God isn't in control. It means a beginning, a middle, and an end to this thing that we call life. Coming back to an earlier point, we are indestructible until God is done with us. When God really is done with us, we're out of here. When will that be? Who knows? It may be years or even decades away, or it may be much closer than that. If you have put your faith in Jesus Christ, you don't have to be afraid of death, because Christ conquered death at the cross when He rose again from the dead. Death died when Christ rose. The resurrection of Jesus from the grave was the very death of death.

I love the way the world changers of Hebrews 11 kept one eye on the distant horizon, regardless of what they went through in their lifetimes. They were looking forward to Heaven.

Abraham walked by faith and "did it by keeping his eye on an unseen city with real, eternal foundations—the City designed and built by God" (v. 10 MSG). The chapter goes on to say, "People who live this way make it plain that they are looking for their true home. If they were homesick for the old country, they could have gone back any time they wanted. But they were after a far better country than that—*heaven* country. You can see why God is so proud of them, and has a City waiting for them" (vv. 14–16 MSG).

God has a City, a Better Country, waiting for you too. If you know Christ in a personal way, you will one day step into His presence and live on and on forever. God will restore what you lost on this earth and will more than make up to you whatever you suffered.

But until that day, walk with Him, and seek to change your world through Him by holding on to your faith.

The Secrets of a World Changer

Therefore, since we are surrounded by such a huge crowd of witnesses to the life of faith, let us strip off every weight that slows us down. . . . And let us run with endurance the race God has set before us. We do this by keeping our eyes on Jesus.

~Hebrews 12:1–2 NLT

When I was a teenager, I dreamed of being an athlete. And with good reason.

It was clear to me that the girls on my high school campus loved and admired the jocks—especially the guys on the football team. So I thought to myself, *Why shouldn't I be on the football team too?*

I had to try. Right off the top, however, I knew I wasn't quarterback material and couldn't learn all those plays. I wasn't big enough to be a lineman or aggressive and mean enough to be a linebacker. I thought maybe I could be a running back or a wide receiver—both glory positions on any football team.

So I went out for football and showed up for all the practices—including the grueling "daily doubles" late in the summer, where we practiced twice a day. It was hard. It was hot. I felt like throwing up on numerous occasions, and I got bruised up a little. But then to my shock and amazement, I made the team. It was so exciting. Maybe one of the best things that had happened to me in my life to that point. I could already picture ordering my letterman jacket—and the impression I would make on the girls.

When all the guys got their heads shaved, I did too. That was a big deal to me at that time. (Now it wouldn't mean much at all.) I had a great head of long blond hair with a little surfer wave going. But I sacrificed my golden locks to be one of the cool jocks.

The day after I got my head shaved, I was called into the principal's office. "Greg," he said, "I'm sorry to tell you this, but you can't be on the football team." (I didn't think he looked very sorry.)

"Why not?" I asked.

"Your grades are too low. You don't have the GPA. Those are the rules."

I can still remember my reply. "Couldn't you have told me this *before* I went through all those practices and shaved my head?"

So I didn't get to play football, but I did get my grades up enough to earn a spot on the track team that spring. And as I mentioned earlier in this book, I liked sprints the best.

I could usually manage a short burst of energy but couldn't keep up in the longer races and faded to the back of the pack.

Through the years I've tried to do a little running now and then, but it gets more and more difficult. And that's even after I got a flashy new pair of running shoes.

I read an interesting statistic that said that 87 percent of those who purchase running shoes never use them for running. So people spend all that money on highly engineered athletic shoes—designed by people with PhDs on a supercomputer somewhere—and just wear them to the grocery store or Costco. But they are looking good!

I don't like exercise, and I'm not naturally inclined to work out. I talk to people who say, "Man, I had a great workout. It felt so good." To me, the only thing that feels good about a workout is when it's over! It is so bad that I don't even like to jog my memory.

Just the other day I was at the gym. I was stretching. I was bending. I was lifting. I was groaning out loud. And that was just getting out of the car.

Even though I stuck it out through football practice to impress the girls, I've never been a real athlete. But I know one thing about people who are. They are very committed.

I've met a few Olympic athletes over the years, some who have even won the gold medal, and I have to tell you, the commitment they have to what they do is next level.

I read somewhere that if you want to be an Olympian and compete for a gold medal, you have to work out four hours a day, three hundred and ten days a year, for at least six years. Now that is commitment.

The author of Hebrews zeroes in on commitment in Hebrews 12, the magnificent chapter that follows Hebrews 11 with its Hall of Faith. In essence, he is looking back at the forty verses of Hebrews 11 and telling us how we should respond in light of what we have just learned from the heroes of faith.

> Therefore we also, since we are surrounded by so great a cloud of witnesses, let us lay aside every weight, and the sin which so easily ensnares us, and let us run with endurance the race that is set before us, looking unto Jesus, the author and finisher of our faith, who for the joy that was set before Him endured the cross, despising the shame, and has sat down at the right hand of the throne of God.
>
> For consider Him who endured such hostility from sinners against Himself, lest you become weary and discouraged in your souls. (Heb. 12:1–3)

What's the preeminent secret of being a world changer? What is the one motive and point of focus that will keep us going even when we become weary or discouraged in the race of life? Here's the answer.

It is Jesus.

We do it for Jesus. We keep running for Him because one day we will stand before Him and see Him face to face.

Let's go back to verse 1 for a moment. Notice that it begins with the word *therefore*. You may have heard this before, but whenever you see the word *therefore* in the Bible, you need to find out what it is *there for*. It will almost always draw on what has just been said in the previous verses or chapters. So, in light of what we have just learned from these heroes of faith in Hebrews 11, and because of their example, let us run with endurance the race stretching out before us.

As we wrap up this book, I want to share with you the six principles of being a world changer that the author of Hebrews, who I personally think was Paul, revealed in Hebrews 12:1–2.

1. World Changers Are in Good Company

Therefore we also, since we are surrounded by so great a cloud of witnesses. (v. 1)

Another translation speaks of "such a huge crowd of men of faith watching us from the grandstands" (TLB).

Not long ago, Cathe and I were invited with a group of Christian leaders to a meeting with the president in the White House. When we went up to the second floor, we walked down a hallway lined with portraits of previous presidents. As we looked into the likenesses of Jefferson, Lincoln, Kennedy, Reagan, and others, it reminded us of our country's rich history, and those who have led us through the years.

As we know so well, those distinguished-looking presidents didn't always live distinguished lives. Many of them were deeply flawed and all of them stumbled and fell short countless times. It's the same with the heroes of Hebrews 11. They weren't perfect either. They weren't always strong, wise, godly, or visionary. But at some point in each of their lives, these men and women stepped out in faith, took hold of God's promises, and made a difference in their world.

In chapter 12, the author of Hebrews is telling us to run like they did, live like they did, step out in faith like they did. This can be done. Bear in mind that the world changers of

Hebrews 11 didn't have nearly as much light and knowledge as we do today. They didn't have Jesus Christ living in their hearts as we do. That is a New Covenant possibility, not an Old Testament possibility. They didn't have the Holy Spirit as a constant companion, indwelling and empowering them, as we do because of the death and resurrection of Christ. They didn't even have a New Testament to read, consider, and memorize. Even so, they pressed on.

Hebrews 11:13 says, "Each one of these people of faith died not yet having in hand what was promised, but still believing" (MSG). How did they do it? They saw it way off in the distance, waved their greeting, and accepted the fact that they were transients in this world. People who live this way make it plain that they are looking for their true home.

We have the same God that they did, and guess what? He hasn't changed one iota. The God of yesterday is the God of both today and tomorrow. He has not grown weaker and He has not lost interest in us. He is as focused on the race you run as He was on the races of Abraham, Moses, and David.

Who then makes up this "cloud of witnesses" seemingly cheering us on in Hebrews 12:1? Are there really people in heavenly grandstands observing our race and shouting encouragement?

I don't know. But I do know we all love receiving some affirmation along the way. Going back to my days of running, I would always notice if there was a pretty girl watching me from the stands. It gave me extra motivation and made me run a little faster.

My granddaughter Allie is now playing soccer, and she has become quite good (if you will accept a grandfather's unbiased opinion). At a recent game, she came up to me during a break. "Papa," she said, "did you see the goal I just scored?"

"Yes, I did, Allie. Way to go. That was so great."

"Where is Nama?" (That's what she calls Cathe.)

"Nama is sick today."

"Papa, did you take a video of me scoring a goal and send it to Nama?"

It's nice to know that someone, somewhere is rooting for you, isn't it?

Is Hebrews 12:1 telling us that we're being rooted on by loved ones who have gone to Heaven before us? Some would say that can't be right, because people on the other side have no knowledge of what is happening on earth. Those who live in Heaven, they say, are totally absorbed in God's glory and worshiping Him and don't concern themselves with happenings in this life. Others take it to the opposite extreme and say that our loved ones are watching us every day. They might even report conversations with those who have passed on and speak of "feeling their presence."

I don't agree with either point of view.

As much as we might like the idea, the Bible doesn't teach that we can converse with those in God's presence or that they somehow guide our steps. If your loved one has died as a believer in Jesus, they are with Him and you will certainly see them again. As David said of his child that died as an infant, "I will go to him, but he will not return to me" (2 Sam. 12:23 NIV).

Does that mean that those in Heaven have no interest or concern about what's happening on earth? I don't think we can say that either. In the book of Revelation, we read these words about a group of martyrs who have died and gone to Heaven.

> They shouted to the Lord and said, "O Sovereign Lord, holy and true, how long before you judge the people who belong to this world and avenge our blood for what they have done to us?" Then a white robe was given to each of them. And they were told to rest a little longer until the full number of their brothers and sisters—their fellow servants of Jesus who were to be martyred—had joined them. (6:10–11 NLT)

These aren't angels; they are regular people like us. They seem to be aware of the passing of time and are tuned in and deeply concerned about the injustices happening on the earth. They want the wrongs to be righted.

Another passage that gives us some pause is Luke 15:7, when Jesus says, "I tell you that in the same way there will be more rejoicing in heaven over one sinner who repents than over ninety-nine righteous persons who do not need to repent" (NIV).

That means there must be a lot of joy and celebration in Heaven, because people are coming to Jesus all the time. Could it be that if one of your loved ones or someone you knew came to Christ on earth you might be aware of it in Heaven? I think it is possible.

After all, we will know more in Heaven, not less.

So then, do you have a cheering section in the heavenly grandstands as you run your race here on earth? We may not know until we get to Heaven ourselves. But I know this much. Those who have gone before us in Christ have set the pace for us and provided us with examples that we can follow.

2. World Changers Are in a Race for Their Lives

Let us run. (v. 1)

One of the reasons why I think Paul may be the author of Hebrews is because of his frequent use of the running analogy.

"I run with purpose in every step" (1 Cor. 9:26).

"I wanted to make sure that we were in agreement, for fear that all my efforts had been wasted and I was running the race for nothing" (Gal. 2:2).

"I will be proud that I did not run the race in vain and that my work was not useless" (Phil. 2:16).

"I have fought the good fight, I have finished the race, I have kept the faith" (2 Tim. 4:7).

"Don't you realize that in a race everyone runs, but only one person gets the prize? So run to win!" (1 Cor. 9:24).[1]

That last Scripture goes directly against the grain of today's culture, doesn't it? We live in an era where we're expected to say that everyone is a winner, whether they are or not. We give out participation trophies just for showing up, telling our kids, "It doesn't matter what the score is. You are a winner!" No, they are not. There is a winner and there is a loser; that's how life works.

God says, "I want you to be a winner in life. I don't want you to be a loser. I want you to run with faith and patience and receive rewards that will make an incalculable difference to you in eternity."

When Allie first started playing soccer she was reluctant, tentative, and not really going for the ball, so I gave her a pep talk. I called her over at the break during a game and said, "Allie, listen. You need 'The Eye of the Tiger.'" I was referring to the Survivor song from the movie *Rocky III* about pressing on and not giving up.

Allie said, "What are you talking about, Papa?"

"Never mind," I said. "You just need to try harder."

Then I had an inspiration. "If you score a goal, Allie, I will buy you a doll." It worked! She scored a goal. Then the next game she scored two goals. Then she scored four goals. And I finally had to say, "I can't give you a doll for every goal anymore. Papa will go bankrupt." But now she doesn't need the extra motivation. She loves competing hard and being cheered on by her family.

You and I are in the race of life, but you are not my opponent. I'm not competing with you, and you aren't competing with me. Your church isn't competing against my church or any other church in town. My opponents and competition, if you will, are the world, the flesh, and the devil. You and I are running with fellow Christians. We each have our own race that God calls us to, but we are running it together.

3. World Changers Run Light

Let us lay aside every weight, and the sin which so easily ensnares us. (v. 1)

You don't want excess baggage in the race of life. You don't want to be running with a heavy backpack slowing your pace and digging into your shoulders. This is hard for me, because

I've been called the original pack rat. Maybe it's because of the way I grew up, but my strong tendency is to save everything and bring as much of my stuff with me as I can manage.

When I travel, I cram way too many things into my bags. At the airport check-in, when I put my suitcase on the scale, the airline people just roll their eyes. It always weighs too much, and each time I have to run between gates in an airport to make a connection, I tell myself that I will never pack that way again. Yes, wheels on luggage is a great concept—until you hit asphalt or carpet. Then the party's over. So here's my new philosophy: If I can't carry it, I shouldn't bring it. (We'll see how long that lasts.)

Is there anything or anyone slowing you down in the race God has placed before you? If I'm running a race and someone keeps grabbing my sweatshirt and dragging me back, is that a productive relationship for winning? If I'm striving to have an appetite for the things of God and somebody keeps feeding me stuff that dulls my taste buds, is that a good thing to eat? With this in mind, I periodically have to take stock of my life, and ask myself about certain activities and relationships. Is this a good thing to do with my limited time? Is this association right for me? Is this person helping me stay close to Christ and inspiring me to keep running and stay on course?

You and I need to run the race with godly people who spur us on—not with ungodly people who slow us down. The bottom line? Look for godly friends. And even more, *be* a godly friend.

One of the world changers we looked at in this book was Abraham. Back in Ur, God told him to leave his family behind and journey to a new land that He would show him.

Abraham obeyed but not completely. He did leave his country and most of his family, but he also hauled along his nephew Lot. Granted, he did it for some worthy reasons, wanting to be a father figure and a mentor to the young man. But Lot ended up being like a spiritual deadweight. His presence brought stress and conflict, and ultimately they had to part ways.

But here's what interests me. As soon as Abraham separated from his nephew, God spoke to him again in a significant way. Sometimes, however good our intentions, we acquire relationships that hurt us, slow us down, or trip us up in the race of life.

We can't let that happen. This is a race we only get to run once, and the implications of how we finish go way beyond the few years of our lives, stretching into the endless realms of eternity.

Again, the first verse of Hebrews 12 says to "lay aside every weight, and the sin which so easily ensnares us." Ask yourself the question, Is this activity or habit or practice in my life dragging me down or speeding me up?

Notice that the Bible here speaks of both weights and sins. There's a distinction. Sin is sin—breaking God's commandments, falling short of His standards, refusing to follow through on what He asks you to do.

But then there's the *weight*. This is whatever slows you down or impedes your race, and it is highly individual. What may be a weight for one person doesn't necessarily mean it will be a weight for someone else. You might say, "Well, I see that Christian over there doing _____, and they seem fine with it. Why can't I do it?" Because you're not that person, and maybe that activity doesn't affect them the same way that it affects you. You might be able to eat one Krispy

Kreme doughnut a week and manage that with flying colors. But I can't go near the place. If I bought a dozen glazed doughnuts for the office on my way to work, I might end up with one walking in the door—and we'd still have to divide it five ways.

4. World Changers Run Hard

Let us run with endurance the race that is set before us. (v. 1)

The term used here for endurance is the Greek word *hypomonē*. It's a word that means perseverance, endurance, steadfastness, or staying power. The Greek definition includes the idea of cheerful, hopeful, perhaps even heroic endurance.

This is a steady determination to keep going, because sometimes our race seems just plain hard, and we become weary. Perseverance, however, keeps us pressing on.

Years ago, Cathe and I went on a long bike ride with a group of friends. My wife is really good on road bikes, and on that occasion, I wanted to go with her. I went out and bought a good bike and—at her urging—picked up a whole biking outfit too. I didn't like all the bright colors and spandex, I didn't like the little clicky shoes that fit into the pedals, and I didn't like the shorts with the padded bottoms that made me feel like I needed a diaper change. But I'd made up my mind to be a good sport, do my best, and try not to embarrass Cathe in front of our friends.

Looking at everyone else as I pedaled along, I started feeling good about how stylish and color-coordinated I was. Besides that, I seemed to have boundless energy. We rode about ten miles, and I was passing everybody. Soon I was in the lead and thinking to myself, *This is so easy. Why do people say this is hard?*

When we reached our destination, however, I found that I'd used up every bit of my energy reserves. I was exhausted and felt as limp as a piece of overcooked pasta. And then it was time to ride the ten miles *back* to our starting point. But I had nothing left! My tank was completely empty. It was so bad that several people took turns riding beside me and pushing on my back to keep me going. It was so humiliating.

After the ride was over, I called a friend on the phone to boast, "I rode twenty miles on a bike today." As we were speaking, I saw Cathe heading out the door with her helmet on. I said, "Where are you going?"

"On a bike ride," she said.

"A bike ride? What do you mean, a bike ride? We just rode twenty miles."

"And I didn't even break a sweat," she replied with a smile.

What we need is endurance and a steady pace, whether we're on a bike or running the race God has placed before us. It's fine to have a massive burst of energy and accomplish great things for the kingdom. But what we really need is determination and staying power. We need endurance.

Where do we get endurance? You may not like the answer. It's in the first chapter of the book of James.

Dear brothers and sisters, when troubles of any kind come your way, consider it an opportunity for great joy. For you know that when your faith is tested, your endurance has a chance to grow. So let it grow, for when your endurance is fully developed, you will be perfect and complete, needing nothing. (vv. 2–4 NLT)

There's that word *hypomonē* again. It is the testing of your faith that produces this strength and staying power. When you go to the gym and lift weights, you realize that you are tearing down your muscles in order to build them up. If you add more weight to your bench press, you may tell yourself, "I can't do this." But you can. You can lower your reps if you need to, maybe doing five instead of ten, but you can keep going. And then when you're successful with five reps, you can aim for ten. You find you can do it, and you wonder why it seemed so hard the week before. And then you add more weight and move up again.

This is the idea in James 1. God will put weights in our lives—problems and disappointments and circumstances that feel heavy to us. And we usually say, "I don't want these weights. I can't do this." But if you want to be strong, you will go through those situations and difficult paths, putting your faith and trust in the Lord. And when you need it, you will find the strength you need—in Him.

5. World Changers Refuse to Live in the Past

Looking unto Jesus, the author and finisher of our faith. (v. 2)

In other words, it's all about focus!

One of my all-time favorite verses in the New Testament is Philippians 3:13–14, where Paul says, "I focus on this one thing: Forgetting the past and looking forward to what lies ahead, I press on to reach the end of the race and receive the heavenly prize for which God, through Christ Jesus, is calling us" (NLT).

Put your past behind you and focus like a laser on what's ahead. Remember that when God forgives you, He *forgets* your sin. How does a God who knows everything forget your sins? I don't know, but that's what it says in the Book: "For I will forgive their iniquity, and their sin I will remember no more" (Jer. 31:34).

So put your past sins behind you, and while you're at it, put your past victories behind you as well.

Some people like to rest on their laurels. They're living in the past, looking at old press clippings, and trying to draw purpose, meaning, and affirmation from long-ago accomplishments. Their profile pic on their Facebook page is from their high school days. Yes, we thank God for what He has done for us and through us in days gone by. But there is a new day before us and a new stretch of the trail we've never run before. It's time to press on.

I love the Lord's words in Isaiah 43:18–19: "Forget the former things; do not dwell on the past. See, I am doing a new thing! Now it springs up; do you not perceive it? I am making a way in the wilderness and streams in the wasteland" (NIV).

A friend of mine told me about a raft trip he took on a wild river in central Oregon. The current was running fast, with beautiful, rugged scenery rushing by. My friend kept turning around to see what they had just passed. But then he realized that by looking behind, he was missing what was just ahead, around each new bend in the river. From then on, he determined to face forward and live in the moment.

That's a good plan for life. Don't spend too much time looking back. Don't take time to indulge regrets. The race is ahead of us, and God is there!

6. World Changers Run the Race of Life for Jesus

*Looking unto Jesus, the author and finisher of our faith, who
for the joy that was set before Him endured the cross, despising
the shame, and has sat down at the right hand of the throne of
God. (v. 2)*

Paul was no doubt thinking of the Olympic Games in Greece
when he wrote these words. In those days, they didn't give
out medals of gold, silver, and bronze. Instead, the winners
would receive a wreath of laurel leaves from the hand of the
emperor himself—the honor of a lifetime.

The idea is that you're in the last lap of a long race and
you're feeling utterly exhausted—like you can't run one more
step. But then, in the distance, you see the emperor in his
gleaming white robe. He's holding out the laurel wreath that
will be placed on your head as you are declared the winner.
With that image filling your sight, you dig down, call on
hidden reserves, and give it all you've got.

So it is for us as Christians. We get bone-weary, footsore,
and discouraged in the race God has set before us. We're
tired of dodging obstacles, tripping over invisible roots, and
fending off attacks. We wake up some mornings and say,
"Really, what's the use?"

Look ahead. Look to Jesus. This is why you run. It isn't
some earthly king or emperor waiting at the finish line but
the Son of God, our Creator, Savior, and Lord. And He isn't
holding out a crown of laurel leaves that will wither in the
sun but a beautiful crown of glory, that will stay with us for
a trillion times a trillion years—just for starters.

This is why, at the end of Paul's life, he would declare: "I
have fought the good fight, I have finished the race, I have

kept the faith. Finally, there is laid up for me the crown of righteousness, which the Lord, the righteous Judge, will give to me on that Day, and not to me only but also to all who have loved His appearing" (2 Tim. 4:7–8).

Here's what I love. Hebrews 12 says that Jesus is not only the *author* of our faith, He is also the *finisher*. We start the race with Him, we end the race with Him, and He runs with us every step of the way. He proves it in Matthew 28:20 when He says, "Be sure of this: I am with you always, even to the end of the age" (NLT).

Look to Jesus. He is the One for whom we run this race. He is the One we sing to when we worship. He is the One we give to in our offerings. He is the One we seek to honor each and every day. We don't do this for applause. We don't do it for notoriety or fame or a thousand likes on social media. We do it so we can stand before Jesus one day and hear Him say, "Well done, good and faithful servant. Enter into the joy of your Lord."

I've heard it said before that God has not called you to be famous but to be faithful.

Look to Jesus. Don't look to circumstances, which can change in a heartbeat. Don't look to people, who will inevitably disappoint you. As author Corrie ten Boom once said, "If you look within, you'll be depressed. But if you look at Christ, you'll be at rest."[2]

You say, "Greg, I can't go on another day." Yes, you can. Get your eyes off yourself. Put a stop to your pity party. Look at Jesus.

"But Greg, people don't appreciate me."

That's okay. You're not in this for people. Do it for Jesus. He will never fail you. He will never let you down and He will keep you running in the race of life.

Keep your eyes on Him, draw your strength from Him, follow His lead, and when the finish line finally comes into view, you will find that you've changed your world . . . just as you step into the next one.

Will You Step Forward?

I have been a Christian now for over fifty years. God has been faithful to me every step of the way.

Yes, people will disappoint you at times and circumstances will overwhelm you. But God is bigger than your problems, and He will complete the work He has begun in your life.

He is the "author and finisher" of our faith.

If you have stumbled and fallen in the race of life, it's time to get back up again. It's not too late. God can turn your mess into a message and your test into a testimony. The Lord can use you to change the world, but your world must change first. Commit yourself to Him today, and invite Jesus Christ to reign over every area of your life. Ask the Lord to help you to be a thermostat, not a thermometer. Take that stand right now!

The world needs changing. Will you step forward like these world changers did?

The world will be a better place if you do.

Notes

Chapter 1 Are You a World Changer?

1. The story is recorded in three out of four gospels: Matthew 9:20–22, Mark 5:25–34, and Luke 8:43–48.

Chapter 2 The World Changer Who Was Out of This World

1. Leonard Bernstein as quoted in Michael Vincent, *Walking in Humility: Seeking to Live the Life God Deserves* (Camarillo, CA: Xulon Press, 2003), 128.

2. Daniel Steingold, "Instabrained: Nearly 6 In 10 Adults Check Social Media At Least 10 Times a Day!" StudyFinds, March 15, 2018, https://www.studyfinds.org/half-americans-use-social-media-ten-times-day/.

3. Jaquelyn Gray, "Teens Check Social Media 100 Times A Day, Says New (And Slightly Unsurprising) Study, But the Reason behind Why They Do It Is Kind of Sad," Bustle, October 7, 2015, https://www.bustle.com/articles/115147-teens-check-social-media-100-times-a-day.

Chapter 3 The World Changer at the End of the World

1. "How Far Can the Human Eye See a Candle Flame?" *MIT Technology Review*, July 31, 2015, https://www.technologyreview.com/s/539826/how-far-can-the-human-eye-see-a-candle-flame/.

Chapter 4 The World Changer with No Forwarding Address

1. XJ Selman, "The 8 Most Hilarious Ways GPS Has Screwed People Over," Cracked, October 14, 2013, https://www.cracked.com/quick-fixes/the-8-most-hilarious-ways-gps-has-screwed-people-over/.

2. Associated Press, "Apple Maps Takes Drivers on a Shortcut across an Airport Runway," *Skift*, September 26, 2013, https://skift.com/2013/09/26/apple-maps-takes-drivers-on-a-shortcut-across-an-airport-runway/.

3. Ian Lind, "Tracking the Migration of the Pacific Golden Plover," iLind (blog), May 4, 2019, https://www.ilind.net/2019/05/04/tracking-the-migration-of-the-pacific-golden-plover.

4. Jacqueline Boyd, "How Dogs Find Their Way Home (without a GPS)," *Conversation*, May 16, 2016, https://theconversation.com/how-dogs-find-their-way-home-without-a-gps-58526.

5. C. S. Lewis, *Mere Christianity*, rev. ed. (New York City: HarperOne, 2001), 136–37.

6. The whole account of Philip and the dignitary can be found in Acts 8:26–40.

7. "This World is Not My Home," Pandora, track 11 on Jim Reeves, *We Thank Thee*, Rarity Music, 1962.

Chapter 5 The Choices of a World Changer

1. Jens Kuerschner, "Test: E.T. and Reese's Pieces," Placedise, May 28, 2014, https://www.placedise.com/blog/test-e-t-and-reeses-pieces/.

2. Brian Viner, "The Man who Rejected the Beatles," *Independent*, February 12, 2012, https://www.independent.co.uk/arts-entertainment/music/news/the-man-who-rejected-the-beatles-6782008.html.

3. Evan Andrews, "10 Things You Should Know about the Donner Party," *History*, January 30, 2020, https://www.history.com/news/10-things-you-should-know-about-the-donner-party.

4. See 2 Chronicles 20:7, Isaiah 41:8, and James 2:23.

Chapter 6 The Temptations of a World Changer

1. Martin Luther, *By Faith Alone: 365 Devotional Readings Updated in Today's Language* (City, IA: World Bible Publishers, 1998).

Chapter 7 The World Changer Who Faced a Giant

1. The whole account of David's anointing can be found in 1 Samuel 16.

2. s.v. "7321: ruwa," *The New Strong's Expanded and Exhaustive Concordance of the Bible* (Nashville: Thomas Nelson, 2010).

3. "What Does the Greek Word 'Tetelestai' Mean?" Bible.org, January 1, 2001, https://bible.org/question/what-does-greek-word-tetelestai-mean.

Chapter 8 The Excuses of a World Changer

1. Charlton Heston, "Guideposts Classics: Charlton Heston's Meetings with Moses," *Guideposts*, July 25, 2013, https://www.guideposts.org/better-living/entertainment/movies-and-tv/guideposts-classics-charlton-hestons-meetings-with-moses.

2. Antonia Blumberg, "Christian Bale Says Moses Was 'Barbaric,' 'Schizophrenic' in Lead Up to 'Exodus' Release," *HuffPost*, October 27, 2014, https://www.huffingtonpost.com/2014/10/27/christian-bale-moses_n_6054336.html.

3. Charles Samuel, "Christian Bale: Moses Was a Terrorist to the Egyptians, a Freedom Fighter for the Hebrews," *IJR*, November 30, 2014, https://ijr.com/2-christian-bale-moses-drones/.

4. Tim Gray, "'Exodus' Star Christian Bale on Playing Moses: 'You Can't Out-Heston Charlton Heston,'" *Variety*, September 30, 2014, https://variety.com/2014/film/awards/exodus-star-christian-bale-on-playing-moses-you-cant-out-heston-charlton-heston-1201317520/.

5. Barry Bouthilette, "Liberate Yourself from Stone," The Walking Coach (blog), May 29, 2017, http://www.thewalkingcoach.net/blog/liberate-yourself-from-stone/.

6. The account of this miracle can be found in Exodus 4:2–5.

Chapter 9 The World Changer Who Faced Long Odds

1. s.v. "4161: poiēma," *The New Strong's Expanded and Exhaustive Concordance of the Bible* (Nashville: Thomas Nelson, 2010).

Chapter 10 "Of Whom the World Was Not Worthy"

1. Warren Wiersbe, *Be Strong (Joshua): Putting God's Power to Work in Your Life* (Colorado Springs: David C Cook, 2010), 190.

2. These accounts can be found in 1 Kings 17:17–23, John 11:38–44, and Acts 20:7–12.

Chapter 11 The Secrets of a World Changer

1. With the exception of 2 Timothy 4:7, all Scriptures in this list are from the NLT.

2. Debbie McDaniel, "40 Powerful Quotes from Corrie Ten Boom," Crosswalk.com, May 21, 2015, https://www.crosswalk.com/faith/spiritual-life/inspiring-quotes/40-powerful-quotes-from-corrie-ten-boom.html.

Greg Laurie is the senior pastor of Harvest Christian Fellowship with campuses in California and Hawaii. He began his pastoral ministry at the age of nineteen by leading a Bible study of thirty people. Since then, God has transformed that small group into a church of some fifteen thousand people. Today, Harvest is one of the largest churches in America.

In 1990, Greg Laurie began holding large-scale public evangelistic events called Harvest Crusades. Since that time, in-person attendance and live webcast views for these events have totaled more than 8.7 million, with 506,644 people deciding to make a profession of faith in Jesus Christ. Laurie was also the speaker at Harvest America in Arlington, Texas, in 2016; with an attendance of 350,000, it was deemed the largest live one-day evangelistic event in US history.

Along with his work at Harvest Ministries, Greg Laurie served as the 2013 Honorary Chairman of the National Day of Prayer, and also serves on the board of directors of the Billy Graham Evangelistic Association. He holds honorary doctorates from Biola University and Azusa Pacific University.

Greg Laurie has a daily nationally syndicated radio program, *A New Beginning*, which is broadcast on more than two thousand radio outlets around the world, as well as a weekly television program.

Greg Laurie has authored over seventy books, including *Jesus Revolution*, *Steve McQueen: The Salvation of an American Icon*, *Hope for Hurting Hearts*, *Johnny Cash: The Redemption of an American Idol*, and his autobiography, *Lost Boy*. The accompanying documentary film, *Lost Boy: The Next Chapter*, has won eight awards at international film festivals. His documentary film, *Steve McQueen: American Icon*, is now out on DVD.

Greg has been married to Cathe Laurie for forty-six years and they have two sons, Christopher and Jonathan. Christopher went to be with the Lord in 2008. Greg and Cathe also have five grandchildren.

TELL SOMEONE

Get equipped to confidently share your faith in Christ with boldness and tact. This free online course will help you use your personal testimony to build a bridge and bring the Good News of Jesus to those around you.

WHAT EVERY GROWING CHRISTIAN NEEDS TO KNOW

As believers, it is important that we grow in our relationship with Jesus Christ. We all should have a desire to be mature, growing Christians. There are key disciplines that we must follow to effectively grow, and Harvest wants to help you understand and establish those habits.

NEW BELIEVER'S ONLINE COURSE

It's important to get off on the right foot in our walk with Christ. And to do that, we must develop good spiritual habits, like reading God's Word and praying daily, attending church regularly, and sharing our faith. In this course, Pastor Jonathan Laurie takes us through the four steps that every new believer needs to take in order to become a strong, mature follower of Jesus.

HAPPINESS ONLINE COURSE

People chase after many things trying to find happiness, things like fame, wealth, and pleasure. But in the end, those things only leave a feeling of emptiness and misery. According to Scripture, the only place to find true happiness is in a relationship with God. In this course, Pastor Greg shows us how to find true happiness by following Jesus and loving others.

GET STARTED AT
COURSES.HARVEST.ORG

HOW THE JESUS MOVEMENT TRANSFORMED THE CHURCH—
and Can Transform YOU

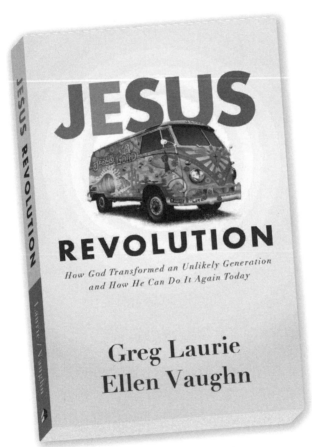

With clarity, humor, passion, and purpose, Greg Laurie and Ellen Vaughn tell the remarkable true story of the Jesus Movement, an extraordinary time of mass revival, renewal, and reconciliation.

BakerBooks
a division of Baker Publishing Group
www.BakerBooks.com

Available wherever books and ebooks are sold.

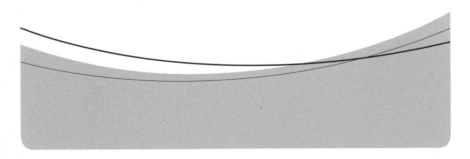